This book is so simple, ye
corporate prayer life of o
encouraged by this resou

Jacob I. King, D.Min.
Senior Pastor, The Church at Liberty Square

As people become more dependent on technology and how they receive information, it has crippled their ability to accurately and patiently research God's precepts which leads them to use worldly habits in seeking a Holy God. *The Prayer Closet* takes us by the hand to a step by step journey that transcends us from an ordinary life to His higher calling for us, to have a deeper, richer understanding of a relational prayer life that seeks to fall in love again and again.

Rev. David Vega, Mission Miami

If there is a quest in your heart for intimacy with God, and something deep within you cries for greater communion with the Father, you must read *The Prayer Closet*. Like iron filings drawn to a magnet, you will be drawn beyond the veil into the holy of holies – into the garden of God. Doug Small's passion is contagious...he is a "keeper of the flame" and invites you to burn with him.

Jeff Farmer, President
Pentecostal/Charismatic Churches of North America

This is such an outstanding book! This volume is a true "hands on" and practical manual to help us engage in meaningful prayer, before His Throne of Grace. I so appreciate Doug's insights, too, to help us move our hearts into a true "Kingdom alignment" as we prepare to seek our Father in our own closets of prayer. Thank You, Lord, for this wonderful resource for all of us who are "standing in the trenches" for You!

Sara Ballenger
Capitol Hill Prayer Partners

Sacred space. Maybe an actual closet. Maybe a recliner. Maybe a kneeling bench in the basement. *The Prayer Closet* book provides the "why" behind the power of a sacred prayer space as well as many biblical and practical ideas that can help you commune when you enter the Lord's presence. If you've ever prayed, "Lord, teach me to pray" this book will help fulfill that heart-desire.

Phil Miglioratti
National Pastors Prayer Network

REFLECTIONS ON THE AUTHOR

Years ago I had the incredible privilege of being impacted by Doug Small's leadership on prayer. I have never been the same. I consider Doug to be one of the foremost authorities on prayer and spiritual awakening in our nation – a real treasure to the church. Doug not only understands the theology of prayer and city movement, but he is tremendous on giving practical leadership to leaders and teams that opens the windows of heaven. You will be deeply helped by Doug's ministry and materials!

Bill Elliff, Senior Teaching Pastor,
The Summit Church, Little Rock|Conway, AR
Pastor/Church Leader of OneCry!

Doug Small and Alive Ministries is one of the most effective prayer movements in America today. He is one of the most effective speakers on prayer in the nation. His deep knowledge of God's Word and his understanding of the principles and practices of effective praying have a tremendous impact. Every time I hear Doug speak I stand amazed at his passion for prayer and his powerful communication of God's Word.

Dr. James D. Leggett, President; Holmes Bible College; Former General Superintendent of the IPHC, President of the Pentecostal World Fellowship, and Christian Churches Together

When our organization wanted someone who understood how to foster a culture of powerful prayer, we turned to Doug Small. He brought biblical, Christ-exalting messages coupled with a winsome spirit and presentation. If you long to ignite lasting impact in your congregation, Doug is a spiritual flame-starter!

Byron Paulus, President,
Life Action Ministries

Doug Small's life is a portrait of passion for Jesus that results from intimacy with God. Many people talk about prayer: Doug Small prays. Drawing upon the lessons God has taught him through devout Bible study and personal experience, this man of God now effectively teaches others about the power of prayer. Whether in the informal bonds of two or three praying together or in a retreat that draws together scores from across a city, his zeal for spending time in God's presence is contagious. I appreciate the influence Doug's teaching on our denomination and on me personally, and I recommend his ministry wholeheartedly.

Dr. Mark L. Williams, Presiding Bishop/General Overseer;
Church of God International Offices

THE PRAYER CLOSET
CREATING A PERSONAL PRAYER ROOM

P. Douglas Small

Alive Publications
A division of
Alive Ministries: PROJECT PRAY

The Prayer Closet
Creating a Personal Prayer Room

ISBN: 978-0-9966379-7-8

Published by Alive Publications,
a division of
Alive Ministries: PROJECT PRAY
PO Box 1245
Kannapolis, NC 28082

www.alivepublications.org

www.projectpray.org

Scripture quotations, unless otherwise indicated are taken from the Holy Bible, New King James Version, Copyright – 1979, 1980, 1982, 1990, 1995, Thomas Nelson, Inc., Publishers.

TABLE OF CONTENTS

1

AN ISSUE OF VALUE:
A PLACE FOR PRAYER

In some Jewish synagogues you find these word inscribed on the wall, "A prayer without the heart, is like a body without a soul."[1] That is a good line to remember for the wall of any prayer room. What we seek is more than a place, more than mere words or even a disciplined, noble routine. It is more than the fact that we pray daily or the function of prayer and its benefits – it is a relationship that, to be transforming, has be centered in the heart. Prayer is not merely something we do, it is someone we are with. And that needs a place!

A growing number of Christians are moving beyond fleeting, self-interested praying – and one of the things that is helping them develop a serious prayer life is the creation of a prayer room.

Ella lived in the same frame house for decades after the death of her husband. It was a simple little house and she was a humble, godly woman. Her generation was a praying generation and Ella had a place of prayer – her back porch. Unadorned. Plain. It was apart from the house, nothing more than the small room through which one passed from the kitchen into the backyard. But it was Ella's place of prayer. She pulled a straight-back chair out of the kitchen, sat it in the small space, and peered through the window of the back door at trees and birds. It was not an awe-inspiring view, but it was her symbolic window on the outside world. With a Bible on her lap, she prayed. For hours, she sat in that simple place of prayer and meditated on God, the things of God, the work of God, and laborers who needed prayer support. The back porch was her sacred space. And you could tell it too. When Ella ministered in

---

1   Brooks, Thomas (2013-09-06). *The Secret Key to Heaven: The Call to Closet Prayer* (Kindle Locations 2057-2058). Titus Books. Kindle Edition.

song, it rocked the church. Behind the natural talent was a supernatural touch – and that came from her prayer times.

Don and Carolyn share a prayer room. It also doubles as a home office, principally as a study for Don, a pastor. Since they also use the office occasionally for interviews and the like, they need to keep the office professional in appearance. So, they frame their prayer cues and covenants and hang them on the wall. They cover some with tapestry banners that are easily reversible – to visitors it is an artful tapestry; beneath it, or pinned to its back is a prayer list. They have a comfortable chair. Ample Bibles. A lamp. Room to lay before the Lord, privacy for extended times with God. The room is large enough for them to use together. At times, they join in prayer there, and, at other times, in the night or early in the morning, one or the other slips into the room for prayer.

Julia is married and has a wonderful husband, and, while he is a believer, he does not share her passion for intercession. Recently, they downsized and moved into a smaller, split-level house. They are empty nesters, and the home into which they moved has three bedrooms. Julia wanted to use one of those bedrooms as a prayer room, but her husband fiercely objected. She complied with his wish to keep the room as a spare bedroom for their children when they visited. As they adjusted to the new home, she kept consolidating storage space until the closet under the stairs was empty – and she claimed it. She cleaned it up, painted it, had an electrical plug added, and furnished it, of course, with miniature furniture. She has a small, low table with a lamp. A bean-bag. A small, low rocking chair. A bookcase. And ample wall space for prayer reminders. She locks herself into the small space for intimate moments with God.

> Prayer is the atmosphere of revelation, in the strict and central sense of that word. It is the climate in which God's manifestation bursts open into inspiration.
>
> ~ P. T. Forsyth, *The Soul of Prayer.*

Robert is a pastor. He and his wife moved into their dream house and, after some time, he felt directed to create a special prayer space. They had a bonus room over the garage and soon discovered that with a bit of imagination, they could convert adjacent attic space and create a rambling prayer room. The room has two dormers, allowing a view of the neighborhood and another of their sprawling backyard, overlooking a meadow. In one alcove, they have created a reading area for mediation and reflection. In the primary area, they have a comfortable chair for times of relaxing and resting. There is also a small desk for study and plenty of room to be on one's face before God. The room is large enough to pace and pray, and yet small enough to still feel intimate! The walls are lined with inspirational images and prayer reminders. They have a growing prayer scrapbook with clippings, photos and lists. There is a globe that allows them to touch the nations, to lay hands on the world in prayer.

Hank and Carinthia lead busy lives – Hank is the assistant principal at a nearby school. He lives in the same neighborhood in which he grew up, the house of his childhood and serves the school he attended as a child; for him, that is quite an honor. However, the house he and his wife share, one in which they are very comfortable, is rather small and there isn't space for a dedicated prayer room. Hank is quite creative and loves gardening – it is therapy for him. At his local hardware store, they were doing a closeout on cute little storage buildings – he bought one and had it placed in the corner of his back yard. It looks like a little, child's playhouse with a small front porch and windows, but Hank uses it as a prayer room. He has installed lights and a small space heater, and it is his getaway for time with God. He sheet-rocked the inside, put a slice of insulation in the walls, a remnant of carpet on the floor, and for him, the place is heaven. A rock walkway connects the back door to the prayer room. The walls are lined with prayer cues. At the beginning of the year, he tries to get his picture made with as many of the kids in the school as possible – and over the years, he has developed quite a collection. He knows the kids by name, and before he meets them in the halls daily, he has met, remembered and prayed for them. Their pictures are on the walls of his little prayer house.

Darcy loves the Lord. She has four children in a three-bedroom, 1,700-square-foot home, and every space is commandeered for some purpose. Peace and quiet are rare, and for her, she realized that the busyness, the sheer pace and demand of life, was threatening her spiritual health. There was no room for a 'special prayer space.' One day, on a tour of garage sales, she spotted a three-panel room divider and was inspired. She bought it for a few dollars, cleaned it up and painted it. It is a free-standing divider that, when opened, is about six feet wide and five feet high. Painted, with appliques, she designed it to blend in with her bedroom décor. When she wants private time with God, she opens the divider, and it shields the chair in the corner of her bedroom. Next to that chair, she has small book caddy, a basket with devotional supplies, tablets, pen and paper. On the front of the divider is a sign, "Mommy needs time with God!" On the back are all the prayer cues and guides that she uses for prayer. "I tell the kids, 'Let me have time with God, and I will be a nicer Mom!' and they are learning that." Like most busy homes with wall-to-wall kids, privacy is hard to find. Darcy is teaching her kids the value of quiet time with God by modeling it.

Pastor Abbott, on the eastern shore of Maryland, prayed by his bedside – that was his place of prayer. And God used him to stir an entire region. Ruth Graham, the late wife of Billy Graham, did likewise. Gigi, the oldest daughter of Billy Graham, said when she stayed with her mother's parents, the Bells, she observed that every morning, her missionary grandfather sat in a particular chair and quietly read his Bible and then knelt, using the chair as an altar. It was like clockwork, every morning, day after day – that was his place of prayer. Armin Gesswein was a great prayer leader. As a young man, he asked a man called Uncle Am, a retired blacksmith and a Methodist lay preacher with a reputation for prayer, to teach him to pray. Uncle Am led him to a barn and up into the hayloft. Armin said, "There, in some old hay, lay two big Bibles – one open." Gesswein noticed there was 'that difference' when he prayed, and the look of an eagle in his eyes – he prayed the Scriptures. "Young man, learn to plead the promises of God!" It is true, we pray ourselves into the will and ways of God by praying the Word of God. Dwight L. Moody once said, "Behind every work of God you will always find some kneeling form." If you want to become a force behind some great work of God, it will begin with times in some dedicated prayer space.

In our daily lives, we have never been more hectic than in this present age. The discipline of daily personal Bible study and prayer time seems almost beyond the reach of many because of the demands upon their time. Yet creating a secret place of prayer is often the beginning point of a deeper personal relationship with Christ. The most important gift we can give our children is our prayers for them – they will have an impact after we are gone. Prayer is the gift that goes far into the future, because it is building a firm foundation that will help them to cope with the increasingly difficult challenges of successful living.

The call of the Holy Spirit to us as the body of Christ has never been more urgent – calling us to return to our roots as a people of prayer. Not *just* prayer, but *prayer as a priority,* a primacy that produces strategic outcomes through prayer. This is the level of prayer that brings God's revelation and answers to the needs of our everyday lives, prayer in which He promises to *"reward us openly"* (Matthew 6:6, KJV). Hebrews declares, *"He that cometh to God must believe that he is, and that he is a rewarder of them that diligently seek him"* (11:6, KJV).

This type of prayer is not content with mere answers; it wants to lay hold of the 'One' who answers. It is not seeking something from Him, not even something noble, it is seeking Him. It partners with the Holy Spirit in advancing the kingdom of God in the earth, in moving forward God's purposes – *"Thy Kingdom come, Thy will be done!"* It is eternity-minded praying. This kind of praying is critical if we are to be healthy Christians, our churches vibrant and our cities impacted. It requires balance in prayer, and this is where the secret place of prayer becomes very strategic. The prayer room allows us to slow down, to hear and pray God's heart, one that is breaking over a lost world. It offers our lives for change – not just the stuff of life for God's management.

The Holy Spirit is calling us to give priority to becoming prayer-saturated, spiritually healthy and productive churches. We cannot be churches of prayer without being people of prayer, and that begins in the home.

Creating a Personal Prayer Room

A prayer room begins with the desire to have a consecrated place to meet with God. While the idea of a personal prayer room connects with many people of prayer, the availability of space may be a challenge. Historically, sincere Christians have found private places for prayer in their home or secluded outdoor spaces. Even old barns and out buildings have been used for prayer. Such places have served people of prayer well over the years. Recently there has been renewed interest in the idea of dedicated sacred space, along with a desire for more enhanced secret places, all a part of the growing and mushrooming prayer movement.

Reports are increasingly common regarding rooms that have been transformed to aid in personal prayer – bedrooms, spare rooms, stairwells, along with the creative use of room dividers, closets and home offices.

Serious intercessors sometimes create a prayer notebook, usually in a loose-leaf three-ring binder into which new pages are easily inserted. Inside the notebook are family photos with prayer tips and guides. Various ministry areas and outreaches of the congregation and denomination to which they belong are included. One intercessor I know has a section on her pastor and his family, then the church elders, the lay-leadership team, pastoral staff and departmental leaders, along with ministry areas. This intercessor is an encourager of other intercessors, and she has identified intercessory peers that have agreed to join her in prayer, to the end that their congregation becomes saturated with prayer. Each of her partner intercessors have taken one of the departments and its leaders as a particular focus in prayer and she supports them – she has duplicated herself a dozen times. She prays for the depart-

> When we go to our meeting with God, we should go like a patient to his doctor, first to be thoroughly examined and afterwards to be treated for our ailment. Then something will happen when you pray.
>
> ~ Ole Kristian O. Hallesby

ments of the church, but perhaps more importantly, she also prays for those doing the praying. It is the reverse principle of Aaron and Hur holding up the hands of Moses; here, Moses is holding up the hands of Aaron and Hur, and a dozen more!

Another intercessor has a special call to pray for her city. She, too, has a notebook with photos and clippings, with lists and directories loaded with names – the community and its leaders. It includes such public service areas as community schools, the law enforcement agency and officers, and elected officials. It has map cut-outs and notes about crime and occult activities, locations of schools and churches, seedy areas and crime spots, drug activity and homicides. She confesses that at one point, she became discouraged; the darkness seemed to overwhelm her. That is when God gave her the gift of friendship with a strategic spiritual mapper. The intercessory peer had wisely learned to not only document the darkness, but also trace the hand of God, His promises, the history of God's work in the city. Now, with more balance, she prays for fresh fire on old altars, for the reopening of wells that once flowed with life-giving spiritual influence, for what God once did in the city to happen again. She has developed some intentional relationships with some young intercessors as well, and she mentors them. Secretly, she is borrowing their energy and optimism.

The last section of another intercessor's notebook includes her denomination's state and national leaders, various missionaries and their projects, Bible schools and medical outreaches, even nations that she has adopted for prayer. Of the hundreds of officially unreached people groups, she has adopted three for prayer, and she searches regularly for fresh information about those groups and evangelistic activity in their behalf.

Each day, these serious intercessors take their prayer notebook to their prayer room or to a quiet place – even when traveling, the book is never left behind – and they are equipped to pray in a very focused manner. "Can you pray without the book?" One smiled and said, "I don't know how!" Of course, they can – and do. But in that notebook is a record of their concerns and their investment in prayer.

Years ago, among the belongings of an elderly intercessor was a private prayer diary with extensive notes about a mission agency in China for which he had consistently prayed. There was a list of twenty mission stations, along with notes enabling him to pray with greater insight into their needs. This was not blind intercession, but studious intercession, out of homework and research. He was an informed intercessor. His prayer life was not random, but systematic, not haphazard, but disciplined. Out of curiosity, a member of his family did a bit of research, contacting the mission stations he had listed in his diary. Were they still open? Were they famishing or flourishing? What stories could they tell? Astonishingly, each of the mission stations had experienced breakthroughs over the years that had led to sustained success. More astonishingly, the exact order in which the breakthroughs had come to each station were the order in which the intercessor had listed them and prayed.[2] Are you the intercessor led to pray for youth? Or children? Or couples? Or singles? Or seniors? Use the church directory to provide visual cues for prayer. Some nursery and children's church ministries snap check-in photos of the children for security and identity purposes – get permission for them to share those with the intercessory prayer team. You may only have a child or baby in the building once, but you can pray for them for years. Who knows the reach of such prayers? Take pictures of places in the city and post them in your prayer room.

- The website pray4everyhome.com allows you to enter your address and get a list of all your neighbors for prayer. You can even connect with other believers who are praying in the same neighborhood.

- Adopt a school for prayer – churchadoptaschool.org.

- Become a trained prayer mentor for your congregation and others, www.projectpray.org/prayer-trainer-program. Launch a Prayer Trainer's Network for learning and teaming in your city.

- Join a number of prayer networks, the Billion Soul Network, billion.tv; the One Cry intercessors initiative, www.onecry.com and Prayerborne, www.praycog.org/prayerborne.

- Find out more about unreached people groups at joshuaproject.net.

- Join the 'Praying Church Movement' and get prayer coaching, consultation, resources and more, www.projectpray.org. Check out more prayer links there.

- Get personal prayer coaching, congregational coaching and consultation, resources and more – from Project Pray. www.projectpray.org/prayer-coaching

- Participate in prayer and vision calls. Contact info@project-

---

2 Duewel, Wesley. *Touch the World Through Prayer* (Zondervan, 1986).

pray.org for more information.

- For you.
- For revival and awakening.
- For transforming your church into a house of prayer.
- For city-reaching efforts.

All of these will contribute to your personal prayer effort. The creative possibilities for your 'prayer room' are limited only by your imagination. Yet the more specifically a room can be reserved for prayer, the more possible benefits there are. Start the process with whatever options you have available; don't wait for the ideal. Use the back of your bedroom or a closet door for your posted prayer lists. Use a consecrated corner. A century ago, the hearth, around an open fire, was where a family gathered for devotions – make the fireplace an altar. Put a Bible on the coffee table and decorate the area with Christian visuals. Consecrate the space and mark it as sacred – the place your family meets with God. Having a visible sacred space, where the family meets with God, could work to change the atmosphere of your entire home.

A prayer room needs to be comfortable and welcoming. While it is a place created specifically for prayer, it can also be a place for study as well. It is a place to pray, to worship, to listen and to be taught in the presence of Almighty God. Choosing a place that is quieter and is available on a daily and regular basis is

> The secret of praying is praying in secret.
>
> ~ Leonard Ravenhill

a top consideration. Most people need space for prayer in the early morning or late at night. That time frame may increase some space options and limit others as possibilities.

Furnish your prayer room with a comfortable chair, a reading lamp, a variety of Bibles and devotional aids. Keep a journal handy, with pen and paper to record insights, ideas, prayer lists and progress. You may want additional worship aids, a means for worship music or audio/video worship/teaching materials. Keep pillows and cushions handy. If you create an altar, you may want to adorn it with artful, inspirational items. Use pictures and maps as focal points and prayer guides.

A prayer room is a place you enter, where you can focus on God and spiritual growth, temperately appropriate, equipped and supplied. The goal is a secret and private place to pray, away from the distractions and interruptions of life. One of Satan's great tools is to keep us from praying. Ephesians 6:16 says that Satan has *fiery darts* (ASV) or *flaming arrows* (NIV) that he hurls at believers. These invisible warheads have the intent of blowing up effective and passionate prayer. There appears to be a zone in which the Evil One sees us as contained. When we attempt to breakout and cross the line of change, we often experience uncanny resistance. When we near breakthrough, on the edge of some victory, we may experience an even greater assault. The goal of the Evil One is always disorientation, distraction and discouragement designed to derail us, decoy or deflect us – and if he can, to destroy us. The darts are coated with fear and guilt, doubt and discouragement, offense and unforgiveness.[3] From such an assault, you need a secret hiding place for renewal.

The Advantages of a Personal Prayer Room

The prayer room is *a place to enter*. Psalm 100:4 declares, *"Enter into his gates with thanksgiving, And into his courts with praise. Be thankful to him, and bless his name."* It is a place to acknowledge and meditate on the awesomeness of God. His name is hallowed – holy.

---

3   Chambers, Sandra (2014-10-07). *Lord, It's Boring in My Prayer Closet: How to Revitalize Your Prayer Life* (Kindle Locations 45-46).

Remember, "Prayer is, at its heart, worship." Worship invites and responds to God's presence. By prayerful worship, we come into relationship and communion with God.

The prayer room is *a place to be still.* Psalm 46:10: *"Be still, and know that I am God…"* In our prayer room, we create a place to come aside and get quiet, to be insulated from the static of the world. In this space, we experience restoration and a refreshing from being in the presence of the Lord. The prayer room is a place to 'soak' in God's presence. The Lord speaks 'peace' when we discipline ourselves in quiet before Him.

The prayer room is *a place to read and meditate on God's word.* No prayer room is complete without a Bible, probably without multiple Bibles, devotionals, reading guides and the like. There is no legitimate prayer apart from the Bible; it is your prayer book. There is no other basis on which we can lay claim to heaven's storehouse than the promises of the New Covenant. Read the Bible. Five chapters a day will get you through the Bible in a year, but that may be less effective than reading a bite-sized passage, over and over, reflecting on it, meditating – and then, using the language of the Scriptures, praying that back to God. Read it, pray it, muse on it through the day, and then come back to it until it comes alive to you, and in you. *"I wait for the LORD, my whole being waits, and in his word I put my hope"* (Psa. 130:5 NIV). Link to online bible guides at www.biblegateway. com.

The prayer room is *a place to seek God's heart.* Prayer is listening as well as speaking. The most important part of the dialogue is not what we say in prayer, but what God might say! Good prayer is putting yourself in a place, physically and spiritually, where you can hear from God. It is a place where we invite God to search our hearts and for us to repent. Here, we ask God to create in us a clean heart and a right spirit. Here, we seek God, come into agreement with Him for our life and those around us. It is the place, to use the language of David, where we "enquire of the Lord." In the context of covenant, on which we pray, out of which we live, prayer partners with God. Illumination comes. Instruction comes. Out of this prayer experience, out of divine authority, the will of God is enforced – first in us, by our submission and obedience, and then through us.

The prayer room is *a place to unburden ourselves*. It is a place where we experience the privilege of asking of God – petition. As we ask, we make "the great exchange," giving God our cares and worries and walking in joy and peace.[4] We talk to the Lord, telling Him everything (1 Peter 5:7; Psa. 44:22). We cry out. We weep. We bring intensity into our prayers. We bring our questions and burdens to exchange for clarity and revelation. He is our provider, our direction, our protection. He meets our daily needs. *"The effective, fervent prayer of a righteous man avails much."* (James 5:16). We trade doubts for faith, weakness for strength, fearful hearts for peace and trust.

The prayer room is *a place to receive and give* (Mt. 6:11-12) and serve. Serving flows from a spirit of forgiveness. It is difficult to serve when holding a grudge or animosity in our hearts. *"For where envying and strife is, there is confusion and every evil work"* (James 3:16, KJV). *"A new commandment I give unto you, that ye love one another; as I have loved you, that ye also love one another"* (John 13:34, KJV). When we walk with Christ in love, we will fulfill all the other commandments. We love others – actively.

The prayer room is a *place to seek God's blessing* (Num. 6:24-26; Psa. 67:1-3), an empowering prayer encounter out of which we bless, according to Romans 12:14. Paul urges us to bless and not curse! According to Hebrews 12:15, we must watch (pray) diligently lest a root of bitterness spring up. Any root of bitterness will greatly hin-

---

4   *The Great Exchange*, a teaching on Phil. 4, by P. Douglas Small (Kannapolis, NC: Alive Publications, 2015).

der us personally and the kingdom of God. Here, we pursue a clean heart and a right spirit in order that our prayers will not be hindered.

The prayer room is *a place of intercession*. It becomes a kind of prayer 'womb.' We give birth to the purposes

> Prayer in its highest form is agonizing soul sweat.
>
> ~ Leonard Ravenhill

of God. Here, we contend for the grace of God to be applied liberally to hearts, whether they are family, friends or just those for whom the Lord has led us to pray. Strategic and focused prayer occurs here. *"Likewise the Spirit also helps in our weaknesses. For we do not know what we should pray for as we ought, but the Spirit himself makes intercession for us with groanings which cannot be uttered"* (Romans 8:26). In this place, we cry out to God and faith is released. Travail is intermixed with praise, with the prophetic declaration of God's word to see the will of God accomplished. Here, the future is changed in prayer. In the Greek language, the image here is of a man of strength and ability stepping under the burden of another human, bearing it, lifting it. It can also be used of a nurse who helps a patient, for example, a child, upholding, supporting, even carrying the other. In our moments of weakness, in prayer, the Spirit carries us as well as our burdens.[5]

Sections of this chapter have been adapted from Carletta Douglas, "Creating Your Own Personal Prayer Room," in The Praying Church Handbook, *Volume 3, Alive Publications. It is used here, with some modifications, by special permission.*

Review Questions:

1. What ideas for creating your own prayer room did you gain from this chapter?

---

5   Brooks, Thomas (Kindle Locations 1349-1353).

rooted in the quality of our relationship with God. Without the relationship, we have no access to the throne room. No right to petition heaven's courtroom. And it is the relationship with God, in Christ, that allows us to reach over the ledge, to offer an *intercessory* hand to someone who is stressed, someone who has fallen, someone who does not have a relationship with God. We, then, through intercession, become an extension of God's love. That extension demands a stronger grip on the upper side than on the lower. It is not out of our strength that we reach, but by God's strength through us.

Defining the Aspects of Prayer

These aspects of prayer, as we noted above, are listed by Paul – *supplications* (petitions), *prayers* (here, a worship word), *intercessions* (meetings with a king), and *thanksgiving*. "*Therefore I exhort first of all that supplications, prayers, intercessions, and giving of thanks be made for all men*" (1 Tim. 2:1).

Supplication is from *deeis*, meaning a request we present to God, a *petition* out of a sense of need. Prayers is *proseuche*. It is a worship word about devotion, used only of approaching God! It speaks of reverence at the heart of communion with God. Our view of God is always at the heart of prayer. Intercession is *enteuxis*, in verb form, from *entugchanein;* it means to meet a king. It is, of course, the idea of praying for others, of standing between God and their needs. Finally, there is the giving of thanks, *eucharistia,* thanking God!

- *Communion* with God is a relational thing – it is at the very heart of prayer. This is the *delight* of prayer, knowing and loving God.

- *Petition* speaks of the *right* of prayer, its privilege. It is also called supplication, from *supple,* meaning to remain flexible and bendable. It is presenting our 'requests' to God and seeking His will.

- *Intercession,* though it involves spiritual warfare, has, at its heart, the goal of *reconciliation.* It speaks of the *duty* of prayer. Its most noble use is in prayer for the lost, those with no vital connection to God.

In each of the aspects, there is a slightly different perspective of God.

- *Communion* sees God as Father. Here, Jesus is the lover of our souls, our bridegroom, our faithful friend. Here is the familial dimension of prayer.

- *Petition* is more structured – formal. It interfaces with heaven as a courtroom. Here, we argue for the purposes of God to prevail on the earth. We present the case for His will to prevail in our lives, our homes, our churches and the earth itself – *"Thy kingdom come, thy will be done in earth, as in heaven…"* We do this over the objection of Lucifer, the accuser of the brethren (Rev. 12:10). Our case is God's case – for righteousness and holiness, His will and purposes to triumph – all according to the promises of the covenant. Here, God is Judge. His decisions are sovereign and final. Mysteriously, by God's grace, prayer affects these sovereign outcomes. Amazing! Jesus, our attorney, intercedes – he represents us in the courtroom of heaven.

- *Intercession* is yet another dimension of prayer. It is a petition in behalf of another. It is a 'friend of the court' brief filed in behalf of another's concern before the court. It goes beyond petition, in that intercession interfaces with heaven as a war room. Here, interventions are launched into the earth. Here, *"Yahweh is a warrior; Yahweh is his name!"* (Ex. 15:3, 14:4; Jer. 20:11; 2 Chron. 20:17). And Jesus is the commander in chief of the army of angels in heaven. Prayer invites God's intervention into the affairs of men. We discover, as someone declared, "God governs the world by the prayers of His people."

Communion is the basis of petition. *"Abide in me…you will ask…"* (John 15:4-7). If there is no communion with God, no ongoing exercise of our covenant relationship, there is no legitimate basis for petition (Prov. 15:29; James 5:16; 1 Peter 3:12). The only right of God is both profaned and disallowed as sacred in the cultural conversation; the right of the Creator to claim and rule the planet He created; the right of Christ to be Savior and Lord is consistently challenged; the will of God is unknown or undiscerned. When it is known, it is ignored and disregarded, even challenged. In our prayer rooms, in intercession, we give voice to the will of God in the earth.

Dallas Willard argued, "Nothing but solitude can allow the development of a freedom from the ingrained behaviors that hinder our integration into God's order."[29] That is, only by prayer, private prayer, time alone with God, can we – by the act of entering into another world in prayer – demonstrate the otherness of prayer, the attachment to God that allows us to be change agents in the present world. Prayer breaks us free of this world; it integrates us in heaven's order and allows us to be an advocate for change. Jesus taught us what we call *the Lord's Prayer*. It is really a prayer for us, and the early church prayed it three times daily. In the opening lines, three simple concerns emerge – that we carry the *name* of the Lord with honor and care, that we hallow His name, live in a manner worthy of the reputation of that name, not sully it in any way, not bring shame or scandal to the name. And, that we recognize the privilege and power in the name. We have switched sides and changed names. Second, the prayer focuses on the kingdom of God, the *rule* and reign of God coming into our lives, our homes, our world. We submit ourselves daily, and throughout the day, to His Lordship. We come under His rule – and, in doing so, we become agents of extending His kingdom. Third, He teaches us to pray for His *will* to be done. So much of our prayer is about our will and attempting to persuade God to do what we ask of Him – but the greater need is to discern His will in each matter, and to bind our will to His will, to give voice, in prayer, to His will for this situation and that. The *name* of God, the

29 Ibid, 160.

rule of the God and the *will* of God – this is the initial template, in a sense, the 'out-of-the-gate' goal of prayer. Every need, every petition, is considered in this light – does it honor and glorify the name of God? Is it consistent with holiness? Does it advance the kingdom of God? Does it further the rule of God in my life, my family, my world? Is it consistent with the will of God, revealed in the Word of God? The name, the rule, the will – this kind of praying changes us, and it changes the world.

Review Questions:

1. Think about the difference between prayer as a habit and a life of prayer.

2. Review the idea of the 'prayer closet' as the storage room of the house – why pray there?

3. Review the story of John Paton, the comments of Cyprian, and the example of the early monks.

4. Review the idea of the prayer closet as a wedding canopy. What are the implications of that symbolism?

5. Consider the prayer closet as a secret place.

4

PRAYING RIGHT:
BEYOND THE PHARISEE AND THE PUBLICAN

E. M. Bounds warns,

The Church is not spiritual simply because it is concerned and deals in spiritual values. It may hold its confirmations by the thousand, it may multiply its baptisms, and administer its sacraments innumerable times, and yet be as far from fulfilling its true mission as human conditions can make it. This present world's general attitude retires prayer to insignificance and obscurity. By it, salvation and eternal life are put in the background. It cannot be too often affirmed, therefore, that the prime need of the Church is not men of money nor men of brains, but men of prayer. Leaders in the realm of religious activity are to be judged by their praying habits, and not by their money or social position. Those who must be placed in the forefront of the Church's business, must be, first of all, men who know how to pray.[30]

Jesus urged prayer in the closet, the secret place. In the same passage, he warned against the practice of the Pharisees, who prayed publically, often with their hands raised. In a stunning contrast, Jesus chose the publican, a tax collector, known for his under-the-table payoffs, his oppression of the poor, as being a better example of prayer than the upright Pharisee. In that day, such a choice was shocking! The privilege of collecting taxes was usually given to the lowest bidder, one who knew he had to make his money from the power of the office – and, as in the case of Zacchaeus, too often it

---

30 Bounds, E. M. *God's Need of Men Who Pray - The Weapon of Prayer.* biblehub. com/library/bounds/the_weapon_of_prayer/iv_gods_need_of_men.htm.

was the poor and powerless that suffered and enriched the pockets of the tax collector. The Pharisees were moralistic and arrogant, but at least they were generally moral. Still, Jesus exalted the publican as doing the best praying. The Pharisee's prayer was self-absorbed. He stood apart, separate, in a holier-than-thou manner, and his prayer was loaded with an exalted view of himself, *"I thank you, God, that I am not a sinner like everyone else. For I don't cheat, I don't sin, and I don't commit adultery. I'm certainly not like that tax collector! I fast twice a week, and I give you a tenth of my income"* (Luke 18:11-12, NLT). The publican stands at some distance as well, but it was due to a respect for the holy space of the temple and the God to whom he prayed. He *"dared not even lift his eyes to heaven as he prayed. Instead, he beat his chest in sorrow, saying, 'O God, be merciful to me, for I am a sinner.'"* The response of Jesus is remarkable, *"I tell you, this sinner, not the Pharisee, returned home justified before God. For those who exalt themselves will be humbled, and those who humble themselves will be exalted"* (Luke 18:13-14, NLT). Chrysostom suggests the plea is "utmost caution against ostentation" – don't pray like a Pharisee.[31]

The Pharisee and Publican – Who Wins the Prayer Contest?

Let's reflect on the passage for a moment. The Pharisee is engaging in the dominant spiritual disciplines – *prayer, fasting, giving.* These control all of life. They are power disciplines.

- First, they help us *draw near* to God by the disciplines of seeking; the chief among these disciplines is *prayer.*

- Second, they help us *yield* to God by disciplines of surrender, of which *fasting* is a critical key.

- Third, they urge us to *reach out* to others by the disciplines of

31 Chrysostom, *Homilies on Gal, Eph, Phi, Col, Thess, Tim, Titus, and Philemon,* biblehub.com/library/chrysostom/homilies_on_gal_eph_phi_col_thess_tim_titus_and_philemon/homily_viii_1_timothy_ii.htm.

service, of which *giving* is the key discipline.

These spiritual disciplines – *prayer, fasting* and *giving* – are 'power connectors' to the Holy Spirit, whose role is to transform us. They are the means by which we give the gift of self as pliable clay to be remade by the Father, into the likeness of Son, according to Scripture, by and through the work of the Spirit. Yet the disciplines are not our goal – our aspiration is Christlikeness (Phil. 3:10). The disciplines themselves do not change us – they position us for change! Our goal is not to be a better pray-er, break a fasting record or top the donor list – rather, it is to be like 'the praying, fasting, giving Jesus.' Yet, while the disciplines are not our *goal*, without them, our *growth* is stunted, dwarfed or non-existent.

The Pharisee had made the disciplines his goal – he *prayed*, he *fasted*, he *gave*! He had arrived. He was at the top of his class in performance. In truth, he had only become self-absorbed in religion. This can happen to all our prayer efforts. The disciplines run along a treacherous narrow ridge between legalism and antinomianism. Their embrace in a legalistic sense only leads to arrogance – we become Pharisees. Their

> Public prayers are of little worth unless they are founded on or followed up by private praying.
> – E. M. Bounds

rejection sends us plummeting into antinomianism, a life with no boundaries and no discipline. Grace inspires us to want to know him and the power of his resurrection! The disciplines are the track that move us toward that goal. The goal itself is a relationship with the ascended and enthroned Christ by the enabling Holy Spirit – one that transforms us.

The publican came in humility. He was without arrogance and pride. He admitted his sinful state and pleaded for mercy, yet for all his straightforwardness, he only arrived at justification. Neither the Pharisee nor the publican are adequate models for prayer. We need the honesty, the integrity of the publican, the lack of self-centeredness and pretention, but to that we must add the spiritual disciplines that provide the track to move humble, forthright people to spiritual maturity. The problem was not with the Pharisee's *praying, fasting* or *giving*, but in his lack of humility. He placed faith in those activities as having the power of change, but that power belongs to God alone – the disciplines are only His instruments for change. Chrysostom said, remarkably, "Suppose that a man were defiled with all manner of sin and enormity – yet humble; and another man enriched with gifts, graces, and duties – yet proud; the humble sinner were in a safer condition than this proud saint."[32] Embracing the discipline of prayer brings change only when we get beyond prayer as duty or drudgery and experience its delight. Persistent, disciplined prayer is the decision to live a life of prayer – because it is a noble and good thing, a healthy and helpful thing, the measure of one's love for the Lord and his longing for the Lord. In prayer, one declares godly intent in a measurable way.

Everything we do as a believer should be done purely, freely, and with a certain level of spontaneity. That assures authenticity. The world's perception of freedom is independent action, radical individualism. No rules. The biblical notion is bounded freedom. Further, it is not merely freedom *from* the guilt and grip of sin, but freedom *to*. We are set free by truth! Trued, changed – liberated into a new alignment with God. It is the pseudo, unbounded freedom of Genesis that enslaves – it is no freedom at all, only an illusion (Genesis 3). True freedom is bounded. God is the ultimate one who is free, but He is bounded; He cannot sin. He cannot tempt us to sin. He is holy and righteous, kind and full of mercy. There are things He cannot, by the decree of His own nature, do! And there are things

32 Brooks, Thomas (Kindle Locations 2353-2355).

He is, out of His nature, not some force or law beyond Him, bound to do! And yet He is God. Freedom, for man, is found not in the absence of boundaries, but inside them; not in the absence of spiritual disciplines like prayer, but by their embrace.

The more you practice prayer in this anchored, daily, habitual way, the more you find prayer being spontaneous and natural during the day. However, if you think that 'chit-chat' prayers can replace the quiet talks in the morning stillness, and, at times, tearful passion, you are trading depth for superficiality in your relationship with God.

Some see the spiritual disciplines – or any 'have-to' or 'ought-to' biblical imperatives – as legalism. We are saved, they argue, and we have no obligation to daily prayer or any other practice. "Salvation is by grace, and grace alone, and grace without works," they assert. Most balanced Christians now see the problem created by such a hyper-grace position. Of course, salvation is by grace alone, but as James, the brother of Jesus, would say simply to us – faith *works*. That is, there are evidentiary manifestations of a faith that is alive in the heart of true believer. One of the clearest is that he talks to God. In truth, it is not an experience, not a set of magic words we call the 'sinner's prayer' that saves us, it is a relationship. And relationship is sustained by dialogue and communication. Yet we are not saved because we pray; we pray because we're saved. We pray because He loves us and keeps drawing us to Him, and we want the quiet and affirming moments we have with Him apart from the world. We pray, not from law, but from love.

What we seem to have developed is what John Piper calls 'half-biblical' people who develop a kind of reverse legalism that militates against doing anything contrary to one's emotional state. The point is that love constrains, and one who is truly in love knows that there are times when one's will is bent, bound to the will of the other, by love. Such moments, though costly, are not regretted. Duty may be involved, but delight drives the experience.

Augustine urged, drawing from Psalm 142, that we should cry out to God in secret, in our closet, shutting the door, and the God who sees in secret would reward us openly. In shutting the door, he believed we were to close off our hearts to God alone, and such private prayer was the means by which we gave no place to the devil. The two great things that needed to be shut out of prayer, Augustine believed, were desire and fear. "Desire only God, and not the world; and fear only the Lord, not what man can do to you."[33]

E. M. Bounds decried the fact that:

> No man is greater than his prayer life. The pastor who is not praying is playing; the people who are not praying are straying. The pulpit can be a shop window to display one's talents; the prayer closet allows no showing off.
>
> – Leonard Ravenhill

> ...many who are enrolled in our churches are not praying men and women. Many of those occupying prominent positions in church life are not praying men. It is greatly to be feared that much of the work of the Church is being done by those who are perfect strangers to the closet. Small wonder that the work does not succeed.[34]

As Bounds notes, "many in the Church say prayers, it is equally true that their praying is of the stereotyped order...they are tame, timid, and without fire or force."[35]

Paul, Jesus and Private Prayer

33 Augustine. *Exposition of the Book of Psalms,* Commentary on Psalm 142; See biblehub.com/library/augustine/exposition_on_the_book_of_psalms/psalm_cxlii.htm.

34 Bounds, E. M. *God's Need of Men Who Pray - The Weapon of Prayer* (Wyatt North Publishing, 2013).

35 Ibid.

In light of this discussion, of the call of Jesus to pray in our closets, what do we do with Paul's call for public prayer? *"I will therefore that men pray every where, lifting up holy hands..."* (1 Tim. 2:8, KJV). Chrysostom noted, "This is not contrary to the other, God forbid, but quite in harmony with it."[36] In fact, there is more here than we commonly see. Actually, Paul here breaks with Jewish tradition in a significant way. He argues against limiting prayer to one place. The great place of prayer for Jewish believers was in their synagogue, and then always praying toward the one true place of prayer, the temple. Paul wants prayer *"in every place,"* which was not encouraged by the Jews. Paul's advice is quite radical, urging us to move from the emphasis on prayer as *a place*, to the *proliferation of prayer everywhere*, as we lift holy hands. Hands free from sin and the taint of the world, hands made pure at the laver of God's sanctifying word – hands that are lifted *"without wrath"* – with no anger, no malice. *"Without doubting"* – hands lifted and prayers prayed in a spirit of faith and expectation.

Paul urges, *"...petitions, prayers [a worship word], intercession and thanksgiving be made for all people,"* but specifically and particularly for *"kings and all those in authority"* – this is the missional, priestly and prophetic dimension of prayer. This is the Church functioning in the role of an ambassador, a representative of heaven's kingdom. Paul claims that such prayers affect the ethos of the community, that inviting God, that praying for our communities and our nation, for those in authority, results in our living *"peaceful and quiet lives in all godliness and holiness."* That is, it affects both the quality of our lives – godliness and holiness – and the nature of our community – peace and quiet. We rarely see such a role for our prayers. Paul says, *"This is good, and*

---

36 Chrysostom. *Homilies on Gal, Eph, Phi, Col, Thess, Tim, Titus, and Philemon,* biblehub.com/library/chrysostom/homilies_on_gal_eph_phi_col_thess_tim_titus_and_philemon/homily_viii_1_timothy_ii.htm..

pleases God our Savior," and what follows is even more telling – an increase in the number of conversions, where people dare to pray publically, lifting holy hands, and blessing the community and those in it. God, *"who wants all people to be saved and to come to a knowledge of the truth"* uses such prayers to accomplish His purposes in calling people to Himself. Thus, when you pray, *"And all things, whatsoever ye shall ask in prayer, believing, ye shall receive."* (Matt. 21:22, KJV). And when you *"stand praying,"* do so with grace, *"forgive, if ye have ought against any"* (Mark 11:25, KJV).

In truth, there is no conflict between Jesus and Paul. Private prayer prepares us for the public function of prayer. Notice that the nature of this public prayer is far beyond the self-absorbed character of the prayer of the Pharisee. This kind of missional praying cares about the city as well as the nation in which we live; it is prayer that seeks a blessing, not a curse. This is prayer that stands between and advocates for God's intervention, for revival and awakening! It is prayer that joins Jesus, who is already praying for our communities, *"For there is one God and one mediator between God and mankind, the man Christ Jesus"* (1 Timothy 2:5, NIV). This is prayer that takes seriously the cross. In fact, it is our answer to the cross, our refusal to allow the death of Christ to not be effectual in the lives of those we live around because he *"gave himself as a ransom for all people"* (1 Timothy 2:6, NIV).

What Paul says next is stunning: *"This has now been witnessed to at the proper time."* The fact of Jesus' death for all men, not just for the Jewish people, but for gentiles, the nations, all people groups, all classes and conditions of people, will now be openly proclaimed. For us, this is almost passé. However, one of the great battles of the New Testament era was the admission of Gentiles into the predominately Jewish Church. Paul saw a global harvest coming. What was not clear in the Old Testament, he shouted, should now be abundantly clear – yet it had not been fulfilled.[37] The gospel had not yet gone to all tribes and tongues, nor has it in our time. The Father desires a harvest of every ethnic tribe and tongue. Thus, we have not yet entered the fullness of this promise, not yet reaped the full coming harvest, not yet experienced the full impact of the work of Christ on the cross in either the church or the world. *"For this purpose,"* Paul declares, *"I was appointed a herald and an apostle – I am telling the truth, I am not lying – and a true and faithful teacher of the Gentiles."* So are we. Somehow, as when we enter the closet and pray, and then proceed to pray everywhere, lifting holy hands, we become intercessory stewards, brokers of the power of blessing, and blessing comes. And the harvest is reaped.

Lifting one's hands and extending them was the priestly posture when blessing the people. The last act of Jesus, recorded in Luke 24:50, was that, in the vicinity of Bethany, *"he lifted up his hands and blessed them."* Jesus moved from time into eternity pronouncing a blessing. Arguably, he is still lifting his hands and blessing. Here, he was fulfilling the prophetic type of Aaron. After the tabernacle had been consecrated, the offerings for sin had been satisfied, Aaron went before the Lord in behalf of the people, and he returned with a blessing. Leviticus 9:22 says, *"Then Aaron lifted his hands toward the people and blessed them"* (NIV). So, when Christ had finished his work on the cross for our sins, he, too, fulfilling the prophetic type, blessed us. He entered the holy places of heaven, not made with hands, and with his own blood sprinkled the mercy seat. And having sat down, he requested of the Father that he send the blessing of the Holy Spirit, who would not only be with his disciples, but in them – in each

---

37 *Barnes Notes on the Bible,* I Timothy 2:6. biblehub.com/commentaries/barnes/1_timothy/2.htm; biblehub.com/1_timothy/2-6.htm; Supplemental Notes.

lively stone, each a part of a living temple. Fire sat upon them – and they were filled with the Spirit! Their heart altars were aflame with God's presence.

First, Jesus is not condemning public praying as much as he is condemning public praying without private prayer roots. The power of public praying is in the strength and depth of the intimacy that comes from private praying.

When Paul speaks of lifting holy hands, he had this specific priestly idea in mind – that is, the power of blessing. When Aaron came out of the holy place, he lifted his hands, along with Moses, and blessed the people. He had entered into the holy place, the hidden place, and then come into the public view before all of Israel, and what he had received in that holy space, he gave to the people – the blessing of the Lord.

Aaron was merely acting out in prophetic type what Christ would literally fulfill when he entered the holy places not made with hands, with his own blood and made the request of the Father that He send the blessing of the Holy Spirit. Now, through the person of the Holy Spirit, Christ would not only to be *with* his disciples, but *in* them. In that moment, in the Upper Room, each lively stone, a part of some invisible altar, indeed, a part of the living temple, had fire sit upon them – they were filled with the Spirit (Acts 2). They became altars, heart altars, aflame with God's presence. Like the priests who gathered the sacred fire when the cloud lifted from the tabernacle and carried in it their fire pan (Lev. 10:1), so we carry the fire. It is the fire of the one altar – the altar in heaven.

We join Christ in prayer, and out of such prayer, out of his work of redemption, we stand as the visible expression of his desire, 'lifting holy hands and blessing the people, the city, its leaders, the unsaved' – and such a blessing releases a stream of grace on our community and results in widespread conversions. " *I desire therefore that the men pray everywhere, lifting up holy hands...*"[38] (1 Tim. 2:8). *"For this is good and acceptable in the sight of God our Savior, who desires all men to be saved and to come to the knowledge of the truth"* (1Tim. 2:3-4).

E. M. Bounds declares,

> God's great plan for the redemption of mankind is as much bound up to prayer for its prosperity and success as when the decree creating the movement was issued from the Father, bearing on its frontage the imperative, universal and eternal condition, *"Ask of me, and I will give thee the heathen for thy inheritance and the uttermost part of the earth for thy possession."*[39]

Review Questions:

1. Contrast the prayer of the publican and the Pharisee.

2. Review the three dominate spiritual disciplines. Discuss how they symbolize and how they serve as the central control points for all of life.

3. What is the difference between the spiritual gifts as a goal and as a track for spiritual growth?

4. Distinguish between duty and delight, between law and love, between 'dead' grace (so-called) and grace that quickens life and love.

5. Paul wants prayer "in every place." So was the public prayer of the Pharisee wrong? What is the relationship between the public and the private life of prayer?

---

38 Chrysostom.
39 Bounds, E. M. *God's Need of Men Who Pray - The Weapon of Prayer.*

5
BREAKIN' THE 'ME' BARRIER:
A BALANCED FRAMEWORK

S o often, our praying begins and ends with ourselves. We pray our narrow slice of pain. We never approach a healthy theology of prayer, which is *thanksgiving, communion* with God, and, while we are experiencing His wonderful presence, *intercession* for others. And the privilege of offering our own needs, *petition,* like a little boy emptying his pockets, or a little girl turning her purse upside down, both saying to God, "This is what I am carrying around, what I dealing with today! Help me, Lord, sort through this." This balance sets our trajectory for the day – a spirit of praise and optimism (thanksgiving), walking in fellowship (communion) and dependence (petition) on God with a sensitivity always ready to pray for others (intercession). We *"pray without ceasing"* (1 Thess. 5:17).

Thanksgiving

In the psalms, we learn that we enter God's *presence* through *thanksgiving.* And it is God's *presence* to which we aspire in prayer – nothing is more important! Prayer is more than words. Our true home is God Himself. We are to *"abide in him"* (John 15:4-7). How do we get there?

As you settle down in your prayer room, you may find it necessary at times to wake up your heart. Thanksgiving is perhaps the best tool for accomplishing that goal. *"We enter his gates with thanksgiving!"* Even if you have a cool heart, especially if you have a cold heart, you embrace *the discipline* of thanksgiving. You force yourself into a review of the goodness of God, specifically His actions in your life. You trace His hand, "You did that – thank you! And I am sure that did not just happen – thank you! And when I was four…you…and without that, my life would not be the same – thank you!" Compel yourself to see God's hand in your life. Give thanks for the gift of life itself – for the capacity to see and smell, to speak and hear, to walk and touch. Don't take God's goodness for granted. *"Every good gift and every perfect gift is from above, and comes down from the Father of lights, with whom there is no variation or shadow of turning."* (James 1:17).

If you embrace the discipline of thanksgiving, you wake up your heart to the goodness of God, and that completely changes the atmosphere for prayer. Here is what happens, from *thanksgiving* you move to *praise*. How is praise different? *Thanksgiving* focuses on *the actions of God* in our behalf. *Praise* focuses on *the God who acts*. Thanksgiving says, "God touched me, saved me, healed me, provided – thank you, Lord." Praise asks, "What kind of God does these kinds of things?" – moving us from the isolated action, to the God who acts: "He is an ever-present, touching God, a saving God, a healing God, and delivering God." This is His nature. He does what He does because of who He is. In praise, we step back and review audibly the characteristics of God, the names of God, the nature of God, His disposition to us and all humanity who come to Him in humility for grace by faith. "God, you are the lily of my valley, the bright and morning star, the first and the last, the Creator and the Redeemer, the lover of my soul. You are Alpha and Omega, you are omnipotent and omniscient, you are holy and merciful – you are my Savior, my Lord, my King. I praise your name." As you review the goodness of God, the characteristics of God, the nature of God and ascribe praise to Him, you will find yourself speechless – and that is not because you have no other words. It is because no other words are necessary!

You have now crossed the threshold from *praise* into *worship*.

"Worship finds its root in the Anglo-Saxon term *weorthscipe*, which evolved into *worthship*, and then to *worship*."[40] "It is the orientation of values. It is the issue of ascribing to God supreme worth."[41] Praise, an expression of worship, involves words, but worship is ultimately beyond words. It is the point at which one is lost in the wonder of God and words are no longer adequate. How do you describe God? How do you talk with Him? Those who had transcendent moments with God found it difficult to give language to the experience – and so it is with true worship. In worship, there is a sudden awareness of 'the presence' of God. The clearest indication of that 'presence' is a sense of God's love. And with that comes peace and joy. Granted, the experience of God's presence, depending on how intense it may be, can be an unhinging experience. On the way to tasting His love, we may be jolted with the reality of our littleness, our sin, our frailty – all to the end that we cast ourselves on His grace and mercy.

> He who has learned to pray has learned the greatest secret of a holy and a happy life.
> ~ William Law

Thanksgiving – to praise. Praise – to worship. In worship – the sense of the nearness of God, the 'presence.' In that nearness – the heart-knowledge of His love, His peace and joy. Now, you can pray. You have not prayed well until you have prayed yourself to silence. Only when you have silence, peace, at your center, can you effectively pray. Anything else is only making noises at the noises of your heart – and that is less than prayer. Paul urged that *"peace was to guard"* our heart, and joy and peace were to be the bookends of healthy prayer (Phil. 4:4-7).

---

40 Martin, Ralph P. *Worship in the Early Church* (Grand Rapids, MI: Eerdmans, 1964), 10.

41 Small, P. Douglas. "In Search of a Pentecostal Liturgy," *Praying Church Handbook, Volume III* (Kannapolis, NC: Alive Publications, 2015), 313.

This may not be an exercise that you do every day! But I have found that prayer is ineffective without a spirit of gratitude. Someone said, "None is more impoverished than the one who has no gratitude. Pride slays thanksgiving, but a humble mind is the soil out of which thanks naturally grow. A proud man is seldom a grateful man, for he never thinks he gets as much as he deserves."[42] James reminds us, *"God resists the proud, but gives grace to the humble"* (James 4:6). You cultivate humility by embracing gratitude. Every need, Paul says, is to be presented, wrapped in thanksgiving, *"...in every situation let your petitions [prayer requests] be made known to God through prayers [worshipful praying] and requests, <u>with thanksgiving</u>"* (Phil. 4:6, ISV). Every situation. Every petition. Every request is to be wrapped in thanksgiving.

Now, you have expressed gratitude, offered verbal praise to God, and found yourself worshipfully in His presence. You sense His love. His peace. Joy. Now, you are in a state of communion with God. Now, you can pray. So, what's next?

Communion with God

The Presence. Don't rush – the presence of God is the most important aspect of the prayer experience. Settle down. Enjoy God's presence. Worship. Consider God's need before you consider your own. For some, that may be a novel idea. God, we know, has no needs. That is true; in one sense, He is utterly other, and we can add nothing to Him. But in the mystery of His ways, beginning in the early pages of Genesis, God comes walking through the garden, looking for fellowship with man (Gen. 3:8). More than sixty times, God appears in angelic form prior to the incarnation – interacting with man, nudging His purposes forward.

---

42 Beecher, Henry Ward. Source: www.quotesdaddy.com/quote/1304609/henry-ward-beecher/pride-slays-thanksgiving-but-an-humble-mind

In the record of Genesis, it is God who speaks first to Adam and Eve; in fact, in the first two encounters, God does all the talking according the Biblical record (Gen. 1:28f; 2:16f). God, it appears, wants to talk us more than we want to talk to Him – and the first word of the Lord to man is that of blessing. Prayer, that moment in which we are engaged by God, is the gateway to blessing. The first Word of God to man in Genesis and the last word of Jesus, is the same, blessing, *"...he raised his hands and blessed them"* (Luke 24:50). The Hebrew word bless is *barak*, and it means knee – thus, to bow, to go to the knee, and in that position, the classic position of prayer, God blesses. The great blessing is that of His presence. Linger there. Soak it in – don't hurry.

The Priority Position. Before you rush into 'God-help-me' prayers or 'God-use-me' prayers, make sure you are in the 'first position' of prayer, centered in the love of God. Prayer is not due to your pursuing God nearly as much as your recognition of His pursuit of you. It is not so much a matter of your love for God – it is the wonderful and enduring fact of God's love for you. "God, I know that You love me, and I love You with all my heart," that's the great center of prayer. Religion begins with our attempt to love God into loving us, or our proving ourselves lovable by the noble example of loving others – both are religion. It is God who loves first, and best. To suggest that we love God into loving us, or that we have proved ourselves lovable – these are inferior to the shocking truth of God's unconditional love for us. If you are convinced that God loves you, faith soars. And if you struggle with whether or not God loves you, your prayer life will be frustrated. It is impossible to have faith in a God whose love you doubt. Most of us do not have a faith problem, we have a love problem. Push back everything else, and settle the issue of God's love for you, and return that love. This is the heart of the prayer.

Pulling Down Strongholds. The great battle in spiritual warfare is not external, it is the one in each of our minds. It is pulling down the strongholds of our own warped thinking (2 Cor. 10:4). Saved, we still think like the world. Casting down imaginations means altering our thinking to align it with heaven. It is thinking about ourselves, about the world and the problems we face, like God thinks about them. What does God say about me? What does the Bible say about this problem? What are God's promises? What are His warnings? How has He revealed Himself to me? Review the names of God from time to time. Pray the principles and the promises of God.

Purity. Forget about advancing with God if there is not an openness to repentance. Prayer is the avenue for God to change us and bring us to health. Spiritual health is impossible without holiness. Holiness is the essence of wholeness. And health cannot be obtained without ongoing repentance. Repentance is an admission of what is right and what is wrong; it is the recalibration of the inner moral compass. With repentance comes redirection. With repentance, we demonstrate humility. With repentance, we evidence not only a respect for the holiness of God, but a hunger for it. Repentance keeps communion with God fresh. It is our apology to God for failings – yet it is not groveling! It is noble sensitivity. It is respectfulness. It is appreciation for holy values and Biblical ideals, for life-giving principles and behavioral benchmarks that characterize the true believer – it is aspiring to Christlikeness. Repentance gives birth to conversion – to change; without repentance, there is no change. Without change, without growth, there is no legitimate prayer life. Martin Luther declared, "When our Lord and Master Jesus Christ said 'repent,' he willed that the entire life of a believer be one of repentance."[43]

Pray Scripture. Nothing will advance your prayer life more quickly

---

43 Burr, Richard A.; Fleagle, Arnold R. (2008-03-03). *Developing Your Secret Closet of Prayer with Study Guide: Because Some Secrets Are Heard Only in Solitude* (Kindle Locations 1799-1800). Moody Publishers. Kindle Edition.

than praying Scripture. Read it and then pray it. Meditate on it – run the passage over and over in your mind and heart. Consider its implications. Review it, and stop along the way. Consider its parts, listen for the voice of God in the Word of God. Let the Scripture speak to you, then muse, question, gasp, consider, align – and take the implication of the passage deep within yourself. Read it. Reflect on it – meditate. And then pray it back to God. Use the language of the passage to create prayer language for yourself. Step into the passage, and pray as if you were in it – use its concepts, its mood, its promises, its call to action and change.

> Fall on your knees and grow there. There is no burden of the spirit that is not made lighter by kneeling under it. Prayer means not always talking to Him, but waiting before Him till the dust settles and the stream runs clear.
>
> –F. B. Meyer

Let's review:

1. *Practice* the presence of God.

2. *Place* yourself in the center of God's love and ask Him to allow that love to multiply in your heart until you love Him and others with the same level of love He has for you.

3. *Perspective.* Dispute the perspectives, the prejudices, the poison in your soul – pull down strongholds in your mind.

4. *Purity.* Align yourself with the character of God, with the testimony of God – what He says about you, about sin, about hope and promise. The battle is in your mind. Repent. Recalibrate.

5. *Pray.* Read Scripture and pray it. Hide it in your heart. Let it change you. Become the Bible to others.

These are the great components of healthy communion with God.

You may bow in prayer, either your body or your head, as Moses did (Ex. 34:8). You may stand in prayer, presenting yourself to God as you would before a king or a judge, as Jesus suggested (Mark 11:25). You may lie in the bed and pray, making the bed an altar – just as the sacrifice was laid on the altar to smolder into the night, you enter into God's rest, and meditate on Him. On the other hand, you may find yourself wrestling in prayer, weeping, groaning in the night in prayer. The psalmist wept until he felt that he was swimming in his bed, watering his couch with tears (Psa. 6:6). You may pray with hands lifted in prayer (Psa. 28:2). The important posture is that of the heart. Daniel knelt (Dan. 6:19), and at another time found himself on his knees and the palms of his hands (10:10). Ezra knelt and lifted his hands, and then sat before the Lord (9:3-5). Jesus fell on his face in prayer (Matt. 26:39).

Intercession

Now, as you sense God's presence, pray for others. Intercede. Keep a list of folks you have committed to pray for – missionaries, the lost, nations, friends and family, community leaders, your pastor, others. You are in the middle, praying, reaching out to touch others. This is a powerful place – a place of impact. The highest calling of prayer is communion with God, but its noblest use is intercession. The heart of prayer is worship, but its edge is mission – and that involves intercession.

Before a missionary successfully ventures through an open door into a new mission field, an intercessor has been there before, pressing the closed door open by prayer. At times, in prayer, you may feel the pain of another and give expression, by means of priestly intercession, to the needs of someone God is helping you love. At other times, you may feel the unction of faith and find yourself boldly declaring the will and Word of God over a person, place or thing. This is the power of prophetic intercession.

In intercession, we also exercise the power of consecration – that's different from sanctification. Only God can sanctify, but to us, He commits the privilege of consecration. There has been a great deal of emphasis on intercession and its connection to spiritual warfare, so much so that some see the terms as synonymous. They are not. Although intercession often involves spiritual warfare, that is not the heart or the goal of intercession. In fact, it is the grand distraction. The heart of intercession, as well as the goal, is reconciliation (2 Cor. 5:19-20; 4:1). Intercession steps into some middle – where a relationship with God does not exist or is under stress due to disbelief, due to spiritual warfare against an individual or entity, due to sickness or some other deprivation, due to confusion or doubt.

In that middle, the intercessor becomes the temporary connection – pleading for the soul of the individual with God, praying about the circumstances and particulars of the situation, and, at the same time, through the mystery of prayer, reaching out in a spiritual, prayerful way, from the prayer closet toward that person. That connection is often magical! Inexplicable things happen. The intercessor has become the earthly connection through which God works in ways we do not understand. They have not left their prayer closet, and yet they have traveled on the magic carpet of prayer, penetrating the dark line of the enemy, rescuing a soul from hell. As Jude says, *"pulling them out of the fire; hating even the garment defiled by the flesh"* (1:23). In the mystery of intercession, we may have set up a barrier of protection; we may have wrapped our arms around a lonely pastor or missionary. We may have appropriated some need that provided critical relief, though another delivered the aid.

The intercessor works in the disputed middle. It is as if there is a dynamic line that is drawn and redrawn between God and men, between the light and darkness, claiming this one and that one, this territory and that – the line, like a battle line, is dynamic, moving. It is the intercessor who penetrates that line and invades the darkness. It is the intercessor who in prayer says, "No!" when the line is redrawn by Satan to claim a soul, a city, or even a church as his own. It would be easy to think, then, that the goal is warfare, a battle over the placement of the line, the pushing back of the darkness – but the goal is not warfare. It is reconciliation of the person or place with God. The line moves not primarily because of the determination of the Evil One, not even because of the intercessor's engagement of the darkness, but because of the heaven-earth connection, because a relationship is formed, for example, between God and a new child. Consecration and sanctification move the line in souls, and cities, in families and factories. It is a blood line, a claim by heaven based on the investment of Christ, now actualized. The light pushes back the darkness. The reconciliation breaks the hold and claim of the Evil One, by the power of the blood covenant, by the rightful claim of God enforced in prayer. Territory is claimed by new altars – in hearts and at homes, in private and public space. This is why there is such a battle over public prayer. The Evil One fights the intercession, and any claim on public space by prayer. He patrols the perimeters, holding his line, attempting to advance the edge of the darkness. So, we are admonished, *"Neither give place,"* *topos*, territory, *"to the devil"* (Eph. 4:27) – the word means a place, a region, a seat; authority. It refers to a locality or an opportunity, a place both in a physical and authoritative sense. *"Don't give him any room!"*

> Pray until you can pray; pray to be helped to pray and do not give up praying because you cannot pray. For it is when you think you cannot pray that is when you are praying.
>
> ~ Spurgeon

Once an intercessor steps into some spiritually or morally disputed territory, some middle, they create a link, by intercession, between God and the disconnected place and party. Doing so, they are likely to see some level of resistance. The goal, however, is not war with the Evil One, though that might be unavoidable. The goal is the rescue of the perishing. The warfare is the great distraction to call our attention away, to detract us from the mission, to get us to give up on this one soul or that one place. We must engage in the warfare without making it the main thing. If we do, we bite the bait – and chase the shadow and lose the focus on the soul needing care. It is by the conversion of souls that we advance the kingdom and move the dynamic line of darkness and light.

In the early chapters of Genesis, God gives Adam the charge to keep or to guard the garden – he is not to give the Evil One any room. The word is *shamar*, to watch (Gen. 2:15), and it is the key word in the Old Testament for intercession. It means, by implication, to take a position with regard to a person, place or thing in the interest of God. The power is in the watching, the alertness and the awareness before God of that person, place or thing. *"The watchman watches in vain unless the Lord watches the city"* – but God watches in our watching! In what may seem a passive function, the intercessor's very existence, his position on the watch, is the means God uses to intervene. We are the satellite dish, catching the beam of heaven, and, by our prayer focus, the energy of heaven is directed here and there, into this darkness and that place. Just the posture of prayer, just the place on the wall, is in itself powerful. *"Could you not watch one hour!"* (Mark 14:37). The concept is found in the Old and New Testament.

Consecration is the means by which we draw a line around a person, place or thing that is within our jurisdictional authority, and, by prayer, we offer that to God, and He works in that consecrated space. He works to sanctify what we consecrate. Everything over which we have jurisdictional authority should be consciously consecrated, given over to God. This draws the line clearly in behalf of another, and in the face of the enemy. Every day, by means of the burnt offering, Israel was consecrated to God anew. The line must be relentlessly redrawn and guarded. We consecrate our land, our living places, our children in dedication, all we have. Consecration is the hedge, it is the blood line of God's claim. It is the bounds into which we intentionally invite the kingdom of God and purposely commit to see His will enforced. Where we have no jurisdictional authority, we use relational authority. And where we have neither jurisdictional nor relational authority or influence, we use spiritual authority, as directed by the Holy Spirit, as kings and priests, and we consecrate cities and towns, peoples and nations – and, by doing so, by praying regularly as intercessors at those drawn lines, we invite God to work within those perimeters to save and transform.

Petition

We think of prayer as a personal, private matter. In one sense, nothing could be further from the truth. On the earth, prayers are private. In heaven – at least on some occasions – they are a part of the public record. There are times when prayer is 'just a little talk with Jesus.' At other times, it is the whisperings of lovers. On occasion, it is time with our wise Father. It can be likened to therapy, to a counseling session, to a consultation with our heavenly attorney.

Still, petition, we must remember, is a legal term. Throughout the psalms, we discover legal language associated with prayer – have mercy, plea or plead, vindicate, hear, as in 'hear ye,' judge, a just cause, my sentence – on and on. When Jesus taught on prayer, on at least one occasion, he used the analogy of prayer as going to court (Luke 18:1-7). Heaven, then, is a kind of courtroom wherein we, like the widow who could not find justice here, in fact, who cannot get a 'hearing' here, press into the courtroom of heaven pleading for justice. We enter our plea, not here, before an unjust judge, but before our heavenly Father. At times, at least on some occasions, our prayers are presented by our attorney of record, Jesus, before the throne of God in heaven. Angels hear them and are sometimes commissioned by God to action as a consequence of God's answer to our prayers. The 24 elders somehow steward the prayers to which God has said, *"Yes, but not yet!"* Prayer thunders in heaven! Its fire crashes onto the earth. God's will is advanced. What an extraordinary privilege.

Imagine getting to heaven and discovering that you are already known because of the prayer life you had on the earth! Imagine learning that your prayers gave God the occasion to intervene not only in the lives of others, but in the affairs of kings and nations. What a powerful privilege to pray!

In Isaiah 43:25-26, we find four stages in the courtroom of prayer! *"I, even I, am he that blots out your transgressions for mine own sake, and will not remember your sins. Put me in remembrance: let us plead together: declare you, that you may be justified"* (AKJV).

- *PUT IN REMEBRANCE.* First – you present your case. You go over the facts. No therapy is as refreshing as that of "pouring out your heart to God in prayer!" This is a review of the facts of your situation, as well as a review of the promises of God – in that intersection of problem and promise, effective prayer takes place.

- *ENTER YOUR PLEA.* Second – God allows you to argue for your own outcome. What is right and just? What is merciful and gracious? What could happen here? Be careful! God isn't tolerant of sin or selfishness. What He is cultivating is our own capacity for discernment, our sensitivity to His will and ways. On the basis of the Biblical principles and promises, we plead for holy outcomes, righteous ends and godly intervention.

- *PLEAD TOGETHER.* Third – prayer is not imposing our will on God. It is a form of discovery. Every trial goes through a process of evidentiary disclosure called discovery. In prayer, we discover the will of God. We may, in the course of searching the Scriptures and our hearts, change our plea. The outcome of prayer is then both objective – results we have sought – and subjective – the changes God desires in us, the awareness that rises in us as we stand before God's throne. Prayer is alignment with God! It involves coming into agreement with God about a matter.

- *MAKE THE DECLARATION.* Fourth – every trial ends with a summary, a closing argument. Prayer should do that as well: "Here are the facts of the problem and the promises. Here is our plea – 'Father, God. We are asking You in this matter to… And this we believe is in accord with Your word and Your will. Further, we are asking for an immediate ruling! For a favorable ruling.'" And then we rest in God.

PRAISE: The final movement in prayer is always praise. The common word for praise in the Old Testament is *halal*, meaning shine. It is a verb, an action – we shine. It is an allusion to God's glory, the effect of being in His presence. By extension, it carries the idea of being a lamp, a light – as we should be out of times of prayer.

As we began, so we end – with a focus not ourselves, but on God. This sets the trajectory for our day – a spirit of praise and worship, sweet communion with God, living in His presence, dependent on Him and sensitive to the needs of others, interceding throughout the day.

The Greek painter Zeuxis introduced innovation into art. His technique involved volumetric illusion by manipulating light and shadow. The new technique affected art in the Renaissance era. He introduced the idea of composites, drawing from several models. He was extremely careful in laying down new lines on canvas and in the process of his work, studying the work from every angle, looking for obvious flaws and faults, optical illusions of inconspicuous design. He was often asked why he was so cautious to release his work and why he viewed it with such severe scrutiny. He responded, "I paint for eternity."[44] So does God. We also pray with eternity in view. Consequently we should draw careful, deliberate lines.

Review Questions:

1. Review the elements of a healthy theology of prayer.

2. Discuss the seemingly contradictory phrase "the discipline of thanksgiving." Review the steps from thanksgiving to the experience of God's love.

3. Do you linger in God's presence? This is one of the purposes of a prayer closet – unhurried times with God. What unhurried encounter with God do you recall that most changed your life?

4. Try pushing back all the 'God help me!' prayers, as well as the nervous 'God use me!' prayers, and center yourself in God's love. What was that experience like? What did you learn?

5. Review the ideas associated with intercession – praying doors open, using the power of consecration, the 'watch,' the position of 'the middle.'

---

44 Brooks, Thomas (Kindle Locations 2958-2961).

6

JESUS – ON PRAYER:
THE PUBLIC AND THE PRIVATE

*But you, when you pray, enter into your closet, and when you have shut
your door, pray to your Father which is in secret; and your Father which
sees in secret shall reward you openly* (Mt. 6:6, AKJV).

J esus referred to the use of a 'prayer closet' two thousand years
ago. He urged, *"...when you pray, enter into your <u>closet</u>...shut
the <u>door</u>, and pray to your Father."* Although Jesus never had
an earthly house of his own with a prayer closet, at least, one we are
aware of, he did choose secluded places for private prayer during
his ministry. Jesus separated himself apart from his disciples to pray
alone (Mt. 14:23). In the morning Jesus arose early before day and
departed into a solitary place to pray (Mark 1:35).

Jesus also prayed publicly. It is important in our creation of private space to recognize that, in creating a *private* space for prayer,
a prayer room, a closet, we are creating a root system for our faith-
life, not merely privatizing it. There are loud voices today, which
suggest, using the 'prayer closet' passages as a pretext, that Jesus ex-
clusively advocated private prayer and only private prayer. Public
praying, these people maintain, is contrary to the teaching of Jesus.
These voices usually cite the example of the Pharisee's prideful public
prayer, which Jesus scorned. However, this is a shortsighted view of
Jesus' record on prayer. A glimpse at the public prayer life of Jesus
shows that his public prayers were ample.

The Intent of the Public Prayers of Jesus

Public prayer is a testimony of faith. In John 11:41-42, NIV, Jesus prayed openly, *"Father, I thank you that you have heard me. I knew that you always hear me,"* and then he added an interesting note, *"... but I said this for the benefit of the people standing here, that they may believe that you sent me."* that is, "I made the prayer public for the sake of these people, who are watching and listening." In this instance, the purpose of public prayer, according to Jesus, was to invite others, by the means of prayer, to believe – *"that they may believe that you sent me."* Public prayer strengthens faith, at least in those who by grace want a connection with God; it incites people to believe and unites those who do believe, binding them together corporately, under heaven, before God. This particular prayer moment precedes the miraculous call of Lazarus back from the dead. Jesus is making it clear, by connecting his public prayer with this miracle, that it is a sign of his relationship with God the Father, and he as Son. The prayer and its effect, resurrection power, both affirm and reveal the nature of the relationship. So it is with us! May we pray and may God act! And may others believe.

Public prayer is the stage on which God might choose to act, to reveal or disclose Himself. On another occasion, a group of Greeks had journeyed to Jerusalem for the feast, and they sought a private audience with Jesus. They approached Philip, *"Sir, we would see Jesus"* (John 12:21, KJV). Philip gained access to Jesus through Andrew. In that context, Jesus prayed, *"Father, glorify your name"* (John 12:28). Suddenly, there was a sound; for some, it was indistinguishable, like the sound of thunder. Others heard a voice, *"Then came a voice from heaven, saying, 'I have both glorified it, and will glorify it again'"* (John 12:28). There were reports that an angel had appeared and spoken. Jesus gave the meaning of the experience, *"This voice,"* an answer to the public prayer, *"came not because of me, but for your sakes."* Again, the public prayer created the context that invited a disclosure of God that opened eyes and strengthened faith.

Public prayer encourages secret believers to go public with their faith. At another point, Jesus had done *"so many miracles...yet they believed not."* Quoting Isaiah, he lamented, *"Who has believed our report?"* Isaiah attributed the lack of faith to *"blind eyes and hard hearts."* Suddenly Jesus erupted into a very public prophetic prayer, *"He that believes on me believes on the one who sent me..."* Buried in the crowd were leaders, among them an undisclosed number from the elite group of 28 chief priests, who were secret believers in Jesus. Sadly, they did not dare go public with their faith in Christ for fear of the consequences. Jesus, by going public, encourages a bolder, more unapologetic face to their faith. This is one of the many reasons we also go public with prayer – to embolden others, to refuse to allow a secretive version of faith in Christ.

Public prayer is a means by which God feeds and nurtures and calls men into covenant. On another occasion of public prayer by Jesus, Mark recorded that Jesus commanded the people to sit down, took seven loaves and prayed, giving thanks. What followed was one of the miracles of the multiplication of the loaves (8:6). Here, public prayer and the miraculous converge, on this occasion as an indication of the compassion and care of God. The feeding of these famished people is reminiscent of the manna in the wilderness. Jesus is presented as the new Moses, leading a new reformation. In a sense, the prayer and the meal is an invitation into a new covenant. It is more than physical bread that we need – the great need is for spiritual bread. With his disciples, as he sat with them for the last supper, there, too, he took bread, blessed it, broke it and distributed it (Luke 24:30; John 6:11). He then framed a new covenant, a new relationship with the Father through Him. A few days later, as a part of the Emmaus

Road experience, he was again breaking the bread. In that moment, the eyes of two discouraged disciples, disillusioned by the crucifixion, were opened and their faith restored. They turned and headed back to Jerusalem with a testimony.

> The story of every great Christian achievement is in the history of answered prayer.
> ~ E. M. Bounds

Public prayer is the open acknowledgement of God. This is almost always the bottom line. By prayer, we publicly acknowledge God. Without it, we ignore Him. Or worse yet, we deny Him. But by it, we open a kind of cosmic door, inviting others to enter into the discourse, to believe – and, ultimately, for God, the Father, to speak or disclose Himself in some sobering or endearing manner, all to the end that faith is born and rises in the hearts of at least some who are present. This was Paul's advice, *"that men pray everywhere,"* publically, lifting up holy hands. Paul suggested that such praying begin with prayer for *"those in authority,"* the people of God standing as very public agents, advocating for the blessing of God on community leaders, with the goal, with the belief, that prayer affects the ethos of the community, allowing for *"peaceful and quiet lives"* (1 Tim. 2:2, NIV). It is also an act of mediation, an extension of the priestly ministry of Jesus Christ – *"that all men might be saved."* Public prayer is an invitation to the people of the community to know God. Also, public prayer, in sufficient quantity and quality, in some mysterious way, affects the very atmosphere of the city. It gives God place by acknowledging Him, by honoring Him, and, in doing so, it engages with divine power for the good of the community and the changing of hearts, one person at a time.

The Effects of the Public Prayers of Jesus

MIRACLES – The miracles out of prayer are real! Jesus really healed people. He supernaturally fed people. He touched them in life-changing ways. He brought peace to the lives of people who were deeply distressed. These miracles also serve as metaphors of the spiritual relationship that prayer offers. If, for example, only our bodies are touched in an encounter with God while our spirits remain deaf and mute, withered and crippled, are we really better off? When Jesus encountered a man who was a deaf and mute, he looked up to heaven, sighed and prayed, and then spoke to the deaf condition, *"Be opened."* The man immediately heard and spoke plainly (Mark 7:34-35). It is for this purpose that Jesus prayed publically and that we continue the practice – that the ears of men be opened to hear, and their tongues be loosed to speak plainly. Prayer, as Paul noted, changes us; it affects speech, and it opens the inner hearts of men to hear (Col. 4:2-5).

BLESSING – Blessing comes in and by prayer – Jesus blessed others by prayer, he demonstrated the use of prayer for the purpose of blessing, ministry, healing and more. Blessing, we should note, is the priestly posture of prayer. It is the noble enactment of God's gracious disposition toward all of us. In blessing, we get to give voice to God's heart for all humanity. In fact, blessing is the first act, the first Word of God to Adam and Eve after creation – *"He blessed them..."* (Gen. 1:28). Moreover, blessing was the last word spoken by Christ before his ascension. He led his disciples toward Bethany, then lifted up his hands and blessed them. Moreover, *"...while he blessed them, he was carried up into heaven."* Here is the great effect of intercessory prayer – the power of blessing (Luke 24:50-53). So, both creation and the new creation, possible only by the creative agency and redemptive work of Christ, are crowned with God's blessing. Not only did Jesus bless, he encouraged his followers to do the same – *"But I say unto you, love your enemies, bless them that curse you…pray for them which despitefully use you, and persecute you"* (Mt. 5:44; Luke 6:27-28).

INTERCESSORY ACTION – As we pray publically, we are to intercede, standing between God and others. The model prayer we pray has others in mind. That prayer, called 'The Lord's Prayer,' is the one Jesus taught his disciples: *"Our Father…Give us this day our daily bread. And forgive us our debts, as we forgive…And lead us not into temptation, but deliver us from evil…"* (Mt. 6:5-15; Luke 11:2-4). Notice the plural pronouns; this is a corporate prayer, not merely a private prayer. That does not mean it cannot be prayed privately; indeed, it is model for prayer, both personal and corporate, but it is explicitly corporate in its desired end. Never once do you find the intensely personal pronouns, "I, me, my." Instead, you find "our, us, we." We claim a relationship with the Father, but never in an exclusive sense – He is *"our"* Father. Prayer for provision – daily bread – must always consider the needs of others – *'give us.'* The prayer is more *transformational* than *transactional* – that is, it is more about *becoming* a forgiving person than merely *receiving* forgiveness, about *being* a giving person, sharing bread, about becoming an agent of help and deliverance for others. Prayer, even personal prayer, cannot be privatized – it always has a relational, corporate, intercessory, others aspect to it. Even when we pray privately, we pray, in a sense, with others in mind. Specifically, we stand between heaven and earth, between Jesus and the others He wants to bless around us and through us.

UNITY – We are to agree, pray with others, and do so in unity with others. In Matthew, Jesus emphasizes the importance of praying with others, *"…if two of you shall agree on earth as touching anything that they shall ask, it shall be done for them of my Father which is in heaven. For where two or three are gathered together in my name, there am I in the midst of them"* (Mt. 18:19-20). Collective prayers are to be offered, even if only by two or three believers gathered anywhere. The most natural thing a handful or large group of believers should do when together is to pray. But it is specifically prayer in his name, that is, the invoking of his name in prayer, that becomes the context in which God's presence settles down in our midst. General delivery prayers don't usually work. Prayers need a name on them. Most religions, some rather boldly, and inflexibly, invoke some deity in prayer. Only Christian cultures seem willing to promote generic praying. When believers invoke the name of God, the name of Jesus, they honor him, they invite him, and they host God's presence. We are the lively stones that provide a living, visible context, an organic temple for God. Prayer in his name creates holy space that honors God, and this should happen in our homes, our factories and office buildings, our schools and campuses, our banks and restaurants, our hospitals and homeless shelters – everywhere, two or three should gather to invite God's presence by prayer in his name.

TRUST – Resignation to the action of God. In Matthew 11:25-26, Jesus was speaking publically to Jewish leaders, and seamlessly, inside the conversation with them, he turned heavenward and prayed, so naturally, *"I thank you, O Father, Lord of heaven and earth, because you have hid these things from the wise and prudent, and have revealed them to babes."* It is a prayer of resignation – he cannot make these people see. That matter, he leaves with the Father, *"...for so it seemed good in thy sight."* This is a lesson in prayer and rest, in leaving the results to God. This is the means by which we resolve relationship frustration – only God can open eyes and reveal things. We can't argue people open to the spiritual dimension. Jesus talks, he shares, he discloses, and at the same

> When God intends great mercy for His people, the first thing He does is set them a praying.
>
> ~ Matthew Henry

time, he prays – and leaves the outcome to the Father, noting that it is the sincere, the child-like who end up 'seeing' and perceiving the spiritual. Notice the natural manner of prayer – in the middle of this encounter, he goes vertical and has a moment with the Father; that relives the tension between his attempt to explain what can only be grasped by the Spirit and the supposedly 'wise and prudent' leaders who, probably, had a rather argumentative and proud disposition. "This one is up to you, Father. I leave this one in your hands."

INCLUSIVE PRAYERS – The Bible says, *"Then were there brought unto him little children, that he should put his hands on them, and pray...And he laid his hands on them..."* (John 12:27-28; Mt. 19:13-15, KJV). What a glorious and culturally innovative idea – Jesus valued children. He wanted them near him. He wanted to touch them. He probably wanted to hear them giggle and laugh with them. He also wanted them to hear him pray for them, bless them – and that should be our goal as well. This was completely contrary to the cultural norm – it was a man's world in which children and women were not to be seen or heard. They were, well, disposable. But not in the world Jesus wanted to create. No child should grow up without hearing their father and mother, a pastor and other leaders, praying a blessing over them. At Simon's house, the famed Pharisee, a sinner woman came and washed the feet of Jesus with her tears and wiped them with her hair, anointing him with spices from an alabaster box. Simon was appalled. *"If this man were a prophet, he would know the kind of woman this is..."* (Luke 7:39) and, by inference, Simon meant, he would not have allowed her to touch him, but Jesus is affirming of this woman, inviting of her worship and devotion, as he is to all of us. He also touched the leper – unthinkable (Mt. 8:3). Rich and poor, Jew and Gentile, young and old, men and women – we are invited to know God, in Christ. He is 'no respecter of persons,' He does not discriminate (Acts 10:34; Rom. 2:11).

GRACE BY PRAYER – Publically, from the cross, Jesus prayed, *"Father, forgive them; for they know not what they do"* (Luke 23:34). In a glorious sense, we are not saved because Jesus died on the cross – we are saved because Jesus died on the cross, *praying*; praying for our forgiveness. In the final hour, he prayed again, *"My God, My God, why have You forsaken me?"* (Mt. 27:46). In his dying breath, he prayed yet again, *"Father, into Your hands I commit My spirit"* (Luke 23:46). Everything he had done to open heaven for humanity had been accomplished. The work was finished. And now, through Christ, *"...we have obtained an introduction into that state of favor with God,"* grace, *"in which we stand,"* that tender, enabling power of His presence that allows us to stand, to stay on our feet (Romans 5:2). After the resurrection, after breaking bread before yet another meal, Jesus prayed again (Luke 24:30). This is the meal of continued fellowship – though he had been crucified, he still showed up to break bread with disciples, and so with us. This is the invitation, now, to his table. This is the promise of his fellowship, of blessing, over broken bread – over open Bibles, with hungry hearts. We have grace by prayer. Grace in prayer. Grace for prayer.

The Outcomes of the Prayers of Jesus

Jesus prayed, sometimes publicly and sometimes privately, and when he did, the gospel narrative often followed with some significant moment. He prayed, and then made some important decision, such as choosing his disciples (Luke 6:12-13). He prayed, and then performed a healing (Mark 7:34-35), and, sometimes, he prayed after a healing (Luke 5:15-16). He prayed before addressing the needs of the hunger of 5,000, and on another occasion, 4,000, with few resources at hand (John 6:11; confer with Mt. 14:19, Mark 6:41; Luke 9:16). He was found praying before he walked on the water

(Mt. 14:22; also Mark 6:46; 15:36; John 6:15). He prayed before Peter's breakthrough revelation that he was 'the Christ' (Luke 9:18). He prayed when the seventy returned, full of joy and with reports of victory – and, arguably, he had prayed as they went on the journey to which he had sent them (Luke 10:21). He prayed before he gave his disciples the lesson on prayer, the model of what we call 'the Lord's Prayer,' though it might more aptly be called 'the disciples' prayer' (Luke 11:1f). He prayed before he ordered the stone rolled away at the resurrection of Lazarus (John 11:41-42). Decisions were made out of prayer times. Healing came following prayer, as did miracles of provision and compassion. He prayed – and things happened that did not normally occur.

Public Prayer with Private Roots

The public praying would have had little effect without the practice of private prayer. There is a private–public dialectic of prayer. The key to the public power is rooted in private times of prayer. Jesus urged, "...*when you pray, enter into your closet, and when you have shut your door, pray to your Father which is in secret; and your Father which sees in secret shall reward you openly*" (Mt. 6:6, AKJV). This is an important key – God often hides. He 'sees in secret,' obscured from our view, not disclosing Himself, and then He rewards openly. The secret to public moments in which God comes out of hiding is found in consistent secret prayer. When nothing seems to be happening in your prayer life, don't measure its impact by what you feel or see as you exit your prayer closet. Consistent daily time with God, even when you don't feel that you are having riveting moments with God, will give birth to surprise ambushes of the Holy Spirit during the day. And there is more. God answers prayer. The Bible contains some 650 prayer requests and some 450 answers – but the real payoff in prayer is not *answers*. We don't even know what to pray at times. The real payoff in prayer is *rewards*. Rewards come, not from seeking the *hand* of God, but the *face* of God. As Hebrews 11:6 notes, *"He is rewarder of those that diligently seek him,"* not merely something from Him, but Him. So much prayer seeks something from God and misses God! He is the great gift – and while He offers Himself, we are satisfied with trinkets. The writer of Hebrews says we are to come to God – that's prayer – and to come in faith, and that is the way we *please Him*. Our current emphasis is to wrap our prayers in faith, in an effort to get God to *please us*. We know that we are growing in our prayer life when the driving dynamic in our prayer life is not to get God to please us, but that we and our life might *please Him*.

In the gospels, at the beginning of the ministry of Jesus, we find the solitary figure wrestling in prayer, with fasting, for forty days. Then in Acts, immediately, we meet corporate prayer, 120 tarrying in the Upper Room for at least a week, waiting on the promise of the Father, the blessing of the Holy Spirit. There are, in Acts, glimpses of private prayer. But it is corporate prayer that is featured, particularly in the early chapters that focus on the church at Jerusalem.

- In Acts 1 and 2, the church is gathered in corporate prayer.
- In Acts 3, Peter and John are seen on their way to a corporate prayer meeting in the temple that is turned upside down by the unexpected miraculous healing of the lame man who sat at the gate called Beautiful.
- In Acts 4:23-31, the church gathered again to pray and rejoice at the release from jail of its leaders. As they prayed, the place was shaken.
- In Acts 6, the leadership of the church, distracted by the needs of the growing numbers of converts, recommitted to corporate prayer and the church began to grow again – on and on.

Only when we pair personal, daily private times with the Father and the practice of corporate assemblies of prayer do we have balance.

In Acts 2:1-4, the fire fell and the city was shaken by the Pentecost Day prayer meeting. Three thousand come to Christ and are baptized (2:41). In one day, the equivalent of six percent of the resident population of the city was saved – granted, many of those were visitors in town for the feast, but the number is still significant.

In Acts 4:4, the number of men who believed in the city had grown to 5,000 – and that did not take into account the wives and children. The number, considering men alone, is ten percent of the population, arguably, overnight, 20-25% of the city had come to believe in Jesus. The threats against the church now intensified, so they gathered in prayer, and the place where they had assembled shook with the power of God – and they were emboldened to stand before the intimidating leadership of the city (4:24-31).

> The coming revival must begin with a great revival of prayer. It is in the closet, with the door shut, that the sound of abundance of rain will first be heard. An increase of secret prayer with ministers will be the sure harbinger of blessing.
>
> – Andrew Murray

In Acts 6, they were distracted by the rapid growth of the church and the needs of the members, but when the leadership recommitted to prayer, the church began to grow again. In Acts 10, Peter had a prayerful, visionary moment on a rooftop in Joppa. That private moment was connected, in the mystery of God's ways, to collective prayer gatherings sponsored by a Gentile soldier in Caesarea, more than thirty miles away. His family, friends and relatives were seeking God. When the private and the corporate converged, God opened the doors to the nations and the Gentile harvest began (10:1-2; 24; 44-45). In Acts 12, Peter was imprisoned, and the church gathered to pray. God sent an angel and brought him out miraculously. In Acts 13, as the church gathered in Antioch, praying, the Holy Spirit birthed the apostolic ministry of Barnabus and Saul. In Acts 16, Paul and Silas were in prison, praying and singing, and God sent an earthquake, breaking off their shackles and opening the jail doors.

This is the dialectic between private and public prayer and the power of the Holy Spirit. As believers pray privately and the church prays corporately, God sends deliverance and provides protection (Acts 16). As they pray, God births missionary activity and the church becomes a sending agency (Acts 13). As they pray, angels are commissioned from heaven (Acts 12). In prayer, new doors are opened into new fields, new hearts are readied to hear the gospel (Acts 10). In prayer, their stagnant condition is dispelled (Acts 6). In prayer, they are emboldened, faith rises, confidence soars and intimidation melts (Acts 4). In prayer, God shakes up a city (Acts 2). This is the power of corporate prayer, but never in the absence of personal prayer. The secret place is ordained of God. *"He who dwells in the secret place of the Most High shall remain stable and fixed under the shadow of the Almighty"* (Psalm 91:1, AMP).

The Amplified Version adds, *"Whose power no foe can withstand!"* Developing a diligent prayer life is vital to living a victorious Christian life. Every follower of Christ should have some place to go to be alone with God to pray. Mornings are an especially excellent time to begin your day in prayer. Or the call "to come apart" could be at any time, whenever the Holy Spirit prompts you. It is difficult to have an effective prayer life without having a designated secret place to pray.

Review Questions:

1. Review the intent of the public prayers of Jesus. How is most of our 'public' praying different? Or similar?
2. What are the 'effects' of the public prayers of Jesus?

3. Discuss the 'outcomes' of the public prayers of Jesus.

4. Review the private–public connection of prayer.

5. Consider the difference between seeking the hand of God and the face of God.

7
TABERNACLE PRAYER
A MODEL

The premier model for prayer in the Old Testament was the Tabernacle. It was the veritable pathway into God's presence – from the world into the Most Holy Place.

The Outer Court – Preparation for His Presence

Half of the tabernacle is dedicated to its courtyard, which is entirely given to preparation for God's presence. The other half, to participation in and with His presence!

The Gate – Praise and Thanksgiving. The prayer cues are: Psalms 148, 149, 150, 98, 100, 105, 107. We enter into God's tabernacle through praise and thanksgiving.

> *Father, I choose to be a person of praise and thanksgiving! To praise, in view of your excellence; out of your grace, and not out of my circumstances. I choose to honor your name, to lift you high by my praises! To carry your reputation as a mighty God!*

The Brass Altar – BLOOD. The brass altar is characterized by blood and fire. It is place of death; literally, it means 'slaughter place.' Three things, all indicated by the different sacrifices prescribed, must die here (Lev. 1-5).

Death of Sin. First, the sin offering (Lev. 4), calls for the death of sin. The substitute lamb would have been slain by the one offering the sacrifice. In placing his hand on the sacrifice, he identified with the lamb, and, in effect, transferred his sins to that lamb. He had no understanding, as we do, that the lamb was Christ. He understood more directly that the wages of sin were death, and the lamb was dying in his place (John 3:16; 1 Peter 1:18-19; Col. 3:5-9; 2 Tim. 3:1-5). Here, we praise God for the 'lamb' Jesus! (Rev. 5:2-10; Heb. 9:11-14; 1 Tim. 1:15; Rom. 5:1-5; 6:6, 14; 3:23-26).

This is the moment in which we repent of any known sin.

Death of Self. The second death is that of self. Having been redeemed, freed from the slavery of sin, we are faced with this question: another has died for us, what will we do with our freedom? The answer is in Romans 12:1-2 (6:4; 6:22; 8:1). We consecrate self to God; it is the only way to stay free. It is the pathway to becoming a yielded vessel. It is the principle of the exchanged life! "Christ died for me; I must now live for him. I yield myself as an instrument of righteousness." As Paul observed, *"I have been crucified with Christ and I no longer live, but Christ lives in me. The life I now live in the body, I live by faith in the Son of God, who loved me and gave himself for me"* (Gal. 2:20, NIV).

This is, in the Old Testament, the burnt offering (Lev. 1). This was not an offering for sin but a free offering, one that advanced the life of the believer. Such an offering is meaningless unless it follows the sin offering. You can never consecrate yourself right with God; you must repent yourself right with God. Attempts at consecration without a respect for the holiness of God are

> We are so egotistically engrossed about God's giving of the answer that we forget His gift of the prayer itself.
>
> - P. T. Forsyth, *The Soul of Prayer.*

pretentious, self-deluding.

Death of Division – The principle of unity and reconciliation. The crowning sacrifice of the five basic offerings was the peace or fellowship offering (Lev. 3). Here was the death of division. Here, the altar was transformed into a table. Here, the worshipper received back a portion of the sacrifice to eat. This is dinner with God! Having come to the altar a sinner; an enemy of God; an alien of righteousness, we are now invited to stay for dinner! (1 Cor. 12:12-14, 25, 27; Eph. 6:15; Rom. 12:9-21; Phil. 2:1-4.)

> *Father, I fear that I take the privilege of your Presence too lightly. I fail to see, that before you, I stand in blood – your blood. This liberty to pray, is costly. Forgive me when I fail to reckon with your beast of righteousness. When I exploit grace. Thank you Father, that you have willed a relationship with me, that Jesus, in love, freely gave himself in the rescue effort to save me from my sin. That the Holy Spirit, having come in the name of the Son, dwells in me. O, how I thank you. May I never take that lightly.*

If we are serious about prayer, God goes after our sin and selfishness. If we yield, surrender, repent and find redirection out of Scripture, by the power of grace, if we stay long enough at the altar, we will end up being fed – having dinner with God. The bloody altar now becomes a place of nurture. The cancer of sin is gone, and we are on the way to health and vigor.

The Laver – Water. The next step toward God is the laver. Here, we pray for purity – we embrace the quest for the 'sanctified life.' The laver was made of mirrored brass and filled with water. One saw the reflection of himself, the need for cleansing, and ready water for purity. Two things were regularly washed – hands (deeds) and feet (habits). Every pass of the laver required a pause for self-examination. Here is the Word (the Bible) as a mirror. In it we see Christ – and in seeing him, we see what we could be, what we should be! (James

4:8; 1:22-25; 2 Cor. 7:1; 6:17; Heb. 10:22; John 17:17). The New Testament calls this the laver of regeneration. Good prayer is over an open Bible, with daily transformation in mind.

Every day, prayer should affect our hands and our feet. It is by *"the washing of the water of the word"* (Eph. 5:26) *"that we can lift holy hands"* (1Tim. 2:8), that our hands are consecrated to legitimately handle holy things. It is by prayer that we leave a holy trail.

> *Lord, cleanse my hands, so that I might legitimately hold holy things. Sanctify me – and let my actions reflect holiness. Cleanse my feet, that I might walk in righteousness, and leave a holy trail for my children.*

The Holy Place – Participation in His Presence

From the court and its natural light, one comes into the holy place and a different light state – the light of the candlestick. The walls were golden and the foundation stones sil-

ver. The ceiling, the *mishkan* – literally, the tabernacle – was predominately blue, but it was embellished with the colors of purple and scarlet on the white linen cloth: blue, the color of heaven; purple, the color of royalty; scarlet, the color of blood; and linen, the color of righteousness. Into the fabric were woven the faces of cherubim as if they were looking down into the holy place, reminding us that the space between heaven and earth grows thin in prayer. Above this colorful ceiling was a layer of ram's skins dyed red, indicating that any meeting with God is under the blood of the lamb.

The Golden Table – Fresh Bread: THE WORD. To the north was a golden table with a crown, a low piece of furniture. It sym-

bolized the word in feed-
ing our souls. Here, the
family of God was invited
to the table of the Lord.
Here, the word incarnate,
Jesus, was broken for our

redemption. *"Take, eat, this is my body!"* (Mt. 26:26; 1 Cor. 11:24).
We are reminded, *"Your word have I hidden in my heart, that I might
not sin against You."* (Psalm 119:11). The table had a crown – kingly
priests gathered here for fellowship. Each Sabbath, fresh bread was
placed on the table. The table was the place where the incense was
stored for the golden altar, as well as the oil for the lampstand. To the
back of the table were attached the silver trumpets, for it was here, at
the table, over the broken bread, a symbol of God's word, that they
most clearly heard the voice of the Spirit. *"Your word is a lamp to my
feet..."* (Psa. 119:105). *"Let this mind..."* (Phil. 2:5). *"Transformed
by the renewing of the mind..."* (Romans 12:2). *"Casting down imaginations...and every thing that exalteth itself against the knowledge of
God..."* (2 Corinthians 10:5-6, KJV).

Every day should involve time at the table.

> *Lord, give me a hunger for your word. Let me hide it in my heart – that
> I might not sin against you. Let it be a lamp to my feet, food for my soul,
> what I offer the hungry folks around me ... Let it be my prayer book. Meet
> me daily at "the table."*

**The Lampstand – Oil: The Ministry of the Holy Spirit – Fruit
and Fire.** To the left, facing west, on the south, was a lampstand. No
one knows the dimensions. It was probably five to six feet high, and
one solid piece of beaten gold in the shape of an almond tree.

- *The Form* **of the Lampstand** – The fruit of the lampstand
  was found in three stages: buds, blossom and fully formed
  almonds. The lampstand is a picture of Christ, yet also of

the Church, and, by extension, we are lights. Our lives by the work of the Spirit, are being molded into the shape of fruit – the fruit of the Spirit. Every day, we should pray, that the life of the Spirit of Christ

will bud, blossom and come to full fruit in us (1 Cor. 13; John 15; Gal. 5:22-23).

- *The Fire* on the **Lampstand** – The lampstand was filled with oil *daily*. Seven flames of fire danced out of the fruit. This is the witness of Christ, the light of the word, and his light through us, by the evident working of the Holy Spirit in the Spirit-filled believer (1 Cor. 2:3-4; 12:7-11; Eph. 5:18-19).

Every day, we are to be filled again with the Spirit. Every day, we are to yield our lives so that we bear fruit, so that others can pull love, joy and peace from the branches of our lives. Every day, we are to trim our wicks, carry out the ashes, the dead, burned places of disappointment.

The table stands in the light of the lampstand, and so the word is understood in the light of the Spirit. Here, in the holy place, in prayer, at the altar of incense, we learn to live by the light of the Holy Spirit, reflected on the bread of life.

Lord, let my life be in the shape of fruit – let it dangle from the branches of my life. And fill me with the Holy Spirit. Light my fire...Let the gifts dance on my life. I pray for authentic character and supernatural power.

The Golden Altar – Incense: Prayer and Worship. Immediately in front of the veil was the golden altar. Twice daily, using live coals from the brass altar, incense was burned. Always at the time of the burnt offering, the time of consecration, morning and night, both altars smoked. The principle is true today – the time of sacrifice, the times when sin dies and self surrenders, when we seek and celebrated reconciliation with God – that is the effective time to light the altar

of incense and get answers to our prayers. The incense, according to Revelation 5:8, represents *the prayers of the saints*. When we pray, heaven's altar smokes. According to John, our prayers, arguably those to which God has said, "Yes, but not yet," are held by the 24 elders of heaven in anticipation of the time when they are cast back into the earth (Rev. 8:3-5; see also 2 Cor. 2:15-16; Eph. 5:1-2; Mt. 6:5-13; Joel 2:17; Psa. 130:1-2; 88:1-2). Here is the powerful end of prayer. This altar has a crown, and it corresponds to the thrones upon which these elders in heaven are seated – prayer has an authoritative, kingly dimension to it.

> *Lord, let my prayer be pure, sweet, spontaneous and broken. Let me offer the depth of myself. Let me pray with fire – with passion. Let me pray according to the Word (Table) and in the light of the lampstand (Spirit). Let my face reflect your glory, evidence that I have been with you.*

We pray through the veil to the God who is enthroned on the Ark of the Covenant, the veritable throne of God. The veil was split, torn, when Christ died on the cross. Its dominate color was white, with the same colors as the *mishkan* – blue, purple and scarlet on a white linen foundation. Embroidered into the veil were cherubim whose images were finished on both sides of the veil, as if they were one with it, peering both into the holy place where priest trafficked and into the Most Holy Place, the secret place, where God alone dwelt. Now, the altar of incense has been relocated and moved inside the veil – by the death of Christ, we have been made insiders, given a privileged place of intimacy with God.

We pray with a reference to the table – the Word, and, by the enabling of the Spirit, in the light of the candlesticks. The Word and the Spirit are our best aids, our great companions in prayer. Incense releases its fragrance only when it touches the fire – passionate prayer, fervent prayer is in view.

The Most Holy Place

Beyond the veil was the Ark of the Covenant – a chest of acacia wood, overlaid with gold inside and out. It had a crown and a cover, a solid plate of gold called the 'mercy seat.' One with the mercy seat, the covering that completed the Ark, were two cherubim, as if rising out of the Ark, their wings touching, some say, forming a throne-like enclosure. In a sense, the Ark represents the Word of God in two parts. The chest was an open and unratified covenant that contained the tablets (the law), the pot of manna and the rod of Aaron that budded. And over them, 'the mercy seat.' Here is God's desire for righteousness (the tablets, the law), and God's promise of provision (the pot of manna) and godly, life-giving authority (Aaron's rod that budded). Here is God's call for holiness of life (the tablets), faith (the daily manna) and a disposition of obedience (the rod of priestly authority). They represent covenant demands – righteousness, faith and obedience.

And here is the good news – these three demands of covenant are covered by mercy. Our covenant with God is not sustained by our obedience, but by the perfect obedience of Christ; not even by our faith, but by his faithfulness; not by our righteousness, but his sinlessness. And yet mercy, such grace, should call righteousness out of us, it should move us to greater faith, it should embolden our obedience.

The God to whom we pray is seated on mercy! The demands of the law are now covered by grace. Yet, this is then a call to greater faith, grace empowered righteousness and a servant heart ready to obey.

The Ark of the Covenant – The Glory. We pass through the torn veil, his flesh, another identification with the cross (Heb. 10:19-20) and encounter the Ark. On the Ark, John says, the lamb is now enthroned with the Father. Here we praise God for the blood-stained mercy seat! And here, we pray for an impartation of God's Glory (Haggai 2:5-9; Hab. 2:14; Joel 2:28-32; Zech. 2:4-5; 10-11). The term Ark, in Hebrew, is coffin. It is a call to total commitment. It is the secret place of the Most High God. *"My life,"* Paul says, *"is hidden with Christ, in God."* In the Ark, I am *"in Christ"* – he is the ultimate Ark of safety, the covering of mercy.

> I am perfectly confident that the man who does not spend hours alone with God will never know the anointing of the Holy Spirit. The world must be left outside until God alone fills the vision…God has promised to answer prayer. It is not that He is unwilling, for the fact is, He is more willing to give than we are to receive, but the trouble is, we are not ready.
>
> ~ Oswald J. Smith

Lord, it is far too easy for us to see only with natural eyes – to fail to see your glory, the invisible throng that joins us in worship, to become either too familiar or too distant. Keep us balanced. Make us mindful that you are the Sovereign One, and we dare not come before you without reverence – or we will send the wrong message to the watching world. Forgive us of less than worthy worship. Having been invited past the veil, may we enter the holiest, knowing we are welcome, indeed, loved – but loving you enough to come in awe of you.

Going Into and Coming Out of the Tabernacle

Let's review – we began by entering the gates and courts with thanksgiving and praise. We stopped at the altar and came under the blood. Sin, self and division died. We paused at the laver made of mirrored brass and filled with water, headed into the holy place, to make sure we had holy hands to handle holy things, and holy feet free of the world's contamination. In the Holy place, at the lampstand, we were filled with fresh oil to assure that fire danced on our lives and fruit dangled from our branches, asking God to work in us in a renewed way. We paused at the table to nourish our souls on daily bread. We knelt at the altar of incense in passionate prayer, asking God for the sweetness of His fragrance to be on our lives. And then, in the Most Holy Place, we crawled into the coffin and died to Christ, that we might be carriers of his glory in a spirit of mercy and grace.

Lord, I leave the Most Holy Place with the glow of your glory, the altar of incense with the fragrance of your presence, with fresh bread from the table, and from the lampstand fruit and fire, clean hands and a pure heart from my encounter at the laver, and at the altar, a sacrificial commitment to serve you. I join you, the lamb, on the altar and give myself to you. And I leave this place – thanking and praising you.

Now we are ready to meet the day, with a contribution from each piece of furniture in the tabernacle.

ARK – *The glow of His glory*
  GOLDEN ALTAR – *The fragrance of His presence*
    LAMPSTAND – *Fruit and Fire*
      TABLE – *Fresh Bread*
        LAVER – *Clean Hands and a Pure Heart*
          BRASS ALTAR – *Gratitude for the Lamb and grace to live above the grip of sin.*
            Out the gate, as I came in, praising!

Review Questions:

1. Review the offerings at the brass altar and their cues for our prayer life.

2. Consider the importance of the laver, of purity as we approach God.

3. Consider the table and the importance of breaking the 'bread' (the Word) as we pray. Consider the implications of the 'form' and the 'fire' of the lampstand.

4. Look at the golden altar of incense as a model for prayer, as a place of prayer – can you picture yourself praying through the veil between the table and the lampstand? What are the implications of such prayer?

5. Review the steps of coming out of the tabernacle. Can you see how such a 'frame of mind' in prayer, out of prayer, would impact not only your time with God, but your life before a watching world?

8

THE PRAYER MODEL JESUS GAVE US

Our Father in heaven, Hallowed be Your name.
Your kingdom come. Your will be done
On earth as it is in heaven.
Give us this day our daily bread.
And forgive us our debts,
As we forgive our debtors.
And do not lead us into temptation,
But deliver us from the evil one.
For Yours is the kingdom and the power and the glory forever.
Amen.

Notice, in this prayer, never once do you find *me, my* or *I.* Instead, you find *our, us* and *we.* This is an intercessory, collective prayer, one we pray with others, and with others in mind. It begins not with us, but with God; not with earth, but with heaven; not with our will, but with a desire to know and do His will. Here, the kingdom of God is found in both the opening and closing lines. The prayer is not about a *transaction* with God, not alone – but about *transformation.* For example, it is not about *being* forgiven, but about *becoming* a forgiving person. It is about sharing bread. It is about deliverance – for ourselves, but not alone, always with others in mind.

In truth, the prayer is not so much meant to be prayed as it is to serve as a template for prayer. There are three divisions to the prayer, nine petitions.

> *Our Father in heaven, Hallowed be Your name.*
> *Your kingdom come. Your will be done*
> *On earth as it is in heaven.*

First, we pray with the GLORY of the Father in mind. Here are three worshipful petitions, related to the *name* of God, the *rule* (kingdom) of God and the *will* of God:

> *Give us this day our daily bread. And forgive us our debts,*
> *As we forgive our debtors. And do not lead us into temptation,*
> *But deliver us from the evil one.*

Second, we pray for the GOOD of the Father's family. Here are three petitions, respectively, for daily *provision*, for *pardon* and for *protection*.

> *For Yours is the kingdom*
> *and the power and the glory forever.*

Finally, we declare the GREAT CERTAINTY of the Father's claim. Here are three final prayerful proclamations – for God's *kingdom*, the manifestation of His *power*, and the revelation of His *glory*.

Though we call this 'the Lord's Prayer,' this is the model of prayer offered by Jesus for New Testament believers.[45] It is really 'the disciple's prayer.'

- The GLORY of the FATHER. We pray that the NAME of God will be revered – *"Hallowed be thy name!"* We pray that the RULE of God will be established – *"Thy kingdom come!"* And we pray that the WILL of God will be done – *"Thy will be done in earth, as it is in heaven!"* In the spirit of His name, under the promises and

> Every work of God can be traced to some kneeling form.
>
> ~ Dwight L. Moody

---

45 I am deeply indebted to an undocumented source for this wonderful, simple outline of the Lord's Prayer. An adaption of this prayer can be found in Elmer Town's *Praying the Lord's Prayer for Spiritual Breakthrough*.

potential offered by the name, in light of the holiness of His nature, we pray for such a God to exert His authority, to extend His rule, and we bind our will to His will, we align ourselves to His purposes.

- The GOOD of the FATHER'S FAMILY! We pray for daily PROVISION – *"Give us this day our daily bread."* We pray for daily PARDON – *"And forgive us our trespasses, as we forgive them that trespass against us."* And we pray for daily PROTECTION – *"Lead us not into temptation, but deliver us from evil!"* Here is the concern for the physical (bread), the psycho-social (the health of the soul) and the unseen spiritual (the Evil One and temptation). Here, the whole person is immersed in prayer.

- The GREAT CERTAINTY of the FATHER'S CLAIM. We proclaim declaratively that the KINGDOM belongs to God – *"For thine is the kingdom."* And we declare that all POWER comes from God – *"And the power!"* And finally, that all GLORY is due God – *"And the glory, forever and ever!"*

The first movement is concerned with the person of God and His holiness – *"Hallowed, holy, is your name!"* This is premier – the fatherly nature of God and His holiness – His unassailable, utterly other uniqueness, His purity and wholesomeness, His perfect 'whole' integrated being – lacking nothing, sufficient to Himself, resplendent, God alone above all gods. Then follows our attestation to His reign – *"thy kingdom come,"* and surrender to His will – *"thy will be done."* Only then do we move to personal needs before turning back, in the doxology, to again focus on God, His kingdom, power and glory. While we pray about needs, the call of prayer is always to move us beyond ourselves and our pain to embrace a life of spiritual poise, between daily needs and cares, and issues of eternal consequences.

"Our Father in heaven": The basis of the divine relationship between God and mankind.[46]

---

46 Adapted from the commentary section on Matthew 6:9-15, from the *Full Life Study Bible;* Donald C. Stamps, Editor, *The Full Life Study Bible* (Grand Rapids: MI: Zondervan Publishing, 1992), 1410-1411.

Heavenly Father, it is a privilege to know You, as Father. In creation, we were the sons of Adam, made in Your image, but through the redemptive work of Christ, we have become children of God. You love us and welcome our fellowship and communion. You desire intimate time with us.

"Hallowed be your name":

Your very name, your nature, is holy. Help us live in accord with Your character and carry Your name with dignity. In a world that disregards, even denigrates and uses Your name in vain, may we hallow it, reverence and honor You. You have disclosed to us Your name – an act of covenant, a disclosure of Your nature, a promise to assist us. You are a holy Father by nature, who understands how destructive sin, disobedience and rebellion are to us. You will correct us, for our own good, when necessary.

Only as we live in a way that glorifies and exalts Your name will the lost see Your value. Help us to make exalting Jesus the priority of our lives; to embrace holiness, and, in doing so, reveal through us the nature of God's goodness.

"Thy Kingdom come":

God, I pray that You would give me grace to come under Your reign, to know Jesus not only as Savior, but also as Lord. I tend to act as my own king, nurturing self-centeredness in my heart – I now repent. I surrender. Let Your kingdom, Your reign, be established in my heart, my home, my church and my city. Jesus, be Lord.

We pray that Your kingdom, Your reign, will be established in the earth. We welcome Your kingly intervention. We pray that we, and the earth itself, will not only reverence You, but submit to You.

"Thy will be done in earth, as it is in heaven":

Let your will be done in my life. Forgive me for trying to get You to do my will. By grace, help me to discern Your will, and allow me the boldness to obey. We pray as Jesus prayed, "Not my will, your will be done," and, in doing so, we bind our will to God's will.

God is glorified when his name is honored worshipfully, when we carry it with integrity and dignity; when the rule of His Kingdom is acknowledged, when his will is done.

Kingdom praying is strategic prayer for the expansion of God's kingdom purposes. It involves prayer for the lost, leaders, churches and communities. Kingdom praying involves intercession for people we will never meet while on the earth, people with whom we are connected only by the mystery of prayer. By our neglect of prayer, of kingdom praying, we allow the kingdom of darkness to both stand and advance without resistance. We are reminded by Paul, *"...the god of this world hath blinded the minds of them which believe not, lest the light of the glorious gospel of Christ, who is the image of God, should shine unto them"* (2 Cor. 4:4). By prayer, we pray that the blinders are removed and eyes are opened, that the lost are freed from spiritual blindness and empowered to respond to the good news of salvation.

"Give us this day our daily bread":

God, we thank You for Your love and the promise of Your provision through the cross for our daily needs. You provided daily manna for Your people in the wilderness, and so in this world, we pray 'for daily bread.' It is 'our' bread – and so help me to share with others. Feed us today, not only our bodies, but nurture our souls and our spirits. We pray for financial needs. We pray for shelter – for those without a home. We pray for healing for bodies racked with pain, without the promise of medical help. We pray for raiment that keeps one warm. You promised to care for the birds of the air, so may we live in faith and trust, free of anxiety. We rest in Philippians 4:19, *"But my God shall supply all your needs according to his riches in glory by Christ Jesus."*

> The truths that I know best I have learned on my knees. I never know a thing well, till it is burned into my heart by prayer.
>
> – John Bunyan

"And forgive us our trespasses, as we forgive them that trespass against us":

God, You have forgiven me – us! What a gift. We were trespassers, with a debt we could not pay, sin-sick, with a disease we could not cure, slaves under a power that we could not break free of – and you saved us. Nothing anyone has done to any of us compares to our offense to You – nothing. Their debts to us are minor compared to the debt of sin we have accumulated with you. We were at war with You and your nature without even being aware of it. At odds with Your nature, engaged in actions that were offensive to You and deadly to us, You rescued us from ourselves. Now, You ask that we give away such grace to others.

Reconciled, our prayers are effective. Holding on to unforgiveness, our prayers are hindered. Bitterness grows in our hearts. We give place to strife and rob ourselves of being blessed and being a blessing. Lord, the wrongs others have done to us are dismissed when we forgive – but they are still wrong, just as the sins that we have committed are still sins, still destructive actions. Only in forgiveness are we freed, and do we free others, from the crippling effects of injustice and invite reconciliation and healing. Give me grace, not only to be humble enough to ask You and others for forgivenes, but also to become a forgiving person.

Now, we examine our hearts. We take inventory of relationships. We pray for a healthy soul. For inner peace. For joy. For love, even for our enemies, especially for our enemies. We are reminded of what Jesus bluntly declared, *"But if you do not forgive men their trespasses neither will your Father forgive your trespasses"* (Matthew 6:15).

"Lead us not into temptation, but deliver us from evil":

Lord, we pray for direction. We can never know what awaits us in any day. So, we submit ourselves to Your care. And we are reminded how, like sheep, we frighten so easily, we follow so blindly. Help me today to be led by You and to be aware that others may be following – so help me take the noble path. I pray for myself and others, that You will hide my eyes from temptations, and if I venture off the path, if I am drawn to evil, deliver me, and in that deliverance, rescue those under my care and influence.

The Evil One has come to steal, kill and destroy (John 10:10). We win our battle by 'submitting ourselves to You, and resisting the devil,' and so he flees. Now, may we submit every idea, every imagination, every decision and desire. May nothing be outside the purview of Your watchful care or the reach of Your intervention. We seek Your protection, direction and provision, the wisdom You have promised to those who love You. We pray for Your Presence.

"For thine is the kingdom, the power, and the glory, for ever and ever.":

The ultimate goal is confidence in the great certainty – the reestablishment of His kingdom in the earth, the manifestation of His power, the revelation and respect due His glory.

As we conclude our time of prayer, we pray that we will be the instruments of advancing the kingdom of God, of living in a way that glorifies God, that reveals His power. Following the counsel of Jesus, we *"seek first the kingdom of God, and his righteousness"* believing that *"all these things shall be added unto you"* (Matthew 6:33, KJV). Here, as in the first moments of the prayer, we again meet the ignored concept of the kingdom. It is in the advance of this kingdom that God is glorified. And it is around the good news of this kingdom that God's power manifests.

Praying the Greats

If you want to come close to praying the heart of God, pray the three 'Greats' of the New Testament.

- The Great Commitment
  Therefore I exhort first of all that supplications, prayers, intercessions, and giving of thanks be made for all men, for kings and all who are in authority, that we may lead a quiet and peaceable life in all godliness and reverence. For this is good and acceptable in the sight of God our Savior, who desires all men to be saved and to come to the knowledge of the truth (1 Tim. 2:1-4, NKJV).

- The Great Commandment
  'You shall love the LORD your God with all your heart, with all

your soul, and with all your mind.' This is the first and great commandment. And the second is like it: 'You shall love your neighbor as yourself.' On these two commandments hang all the Law and the Prophets (Mat. 22:37-40, NKJV).

• The Great Commission
Go therefore and make disciples of all the nations, baptizing them in the name of the Father and of the Son and of the Holy Spirit, teaching them to observe all things that I have commanded you; and lo, I am with you always, even to the end of the age. Amen. (Mat. 28:18-20, NKJV).

As we pray (the Great Commitment), we are changed, transformed, made to love like Christ (the Great Commandment), and only then can we fulfill our obligation to share the gospel with the nations (the Great Commission). We

> I will not let thee go, except thou bless me.
> ~ Jacob

have been doing 'Great Commission' work for years (sharing), but now we are learning to partner it with 'Great Commandment' deeds, to share the gospel in the spirit of love and compassion (caring). That is possible only out of the energy of the Holy Spirit, the 'Great Commitment' (praying). These three – praying, caring, sharing – must be partnered. We pray until we feel the care of God reaching to and through us to others, and as we care, by divine grace, we find the doors to hearts open, and we share the gospel.

Review Questions:

1. Review 'the prayer' in terms of transformation by God and not merely a transaction with God.

2. Rehearse the outline of 'the prayer' in this chapter – the *glory*, the *good* of the Father's family, the *great certainty*.

3. Look at the aspects of the *name*, the *rule* (kingdom) and the *will* of God.

4. Review the aspects of *provision*, *pardon* and *protection*.

5. Review the three 'Greats!'

9
THIN PLACES:
NOT THE PLACE, IT'S THE PERSON

The early Celtic people who lived in the British Isles believed that certain *places* allowed one to be closer to God. Most of us feel that way. That is, there are certain places where we sense more clearly the presence of God. It may be because of the splendor and awe of some majestic natural scene. Still others know a garden or secret place where there is a sense of sacredness that makes communion with God sweet and easy. These places are often called 'thin places.' The Celtics coined the term to describe a place where a person experienced what seemed to be only a thin divide between the past, present and future timelessness; and, of course, between heaven and earth.

Today, the term 'open heaven' is used to express a similar concept, in which the veil that separates the spiritual and the natural, this world and the next, is so sheer you can almost step through, and God often does. Such moments become the occasion of transcendent prayer experiences – moments when the world on top of this world becomes more real than the seen and felt world.

Isaiah recorded such a moment (Isa. 6), where the throne of God and the scenes of *seraphim* and the heavenly altar were so real, he felt the earth around him tremble, he heard voices and saw the fire on heaven's altar. Paul was caught up into the third heaven (2 Cor. 12:2). The experience was so unearthly that Paul had difficulty discerning whether he was dead or alive, in or out of his body, when it happened. Peter, on the rooftop, had a vision so real, the food on the sheet lowered from the spirit realm seemed tangible and edible (Acts 10:9-16). John, too, on the isle of Patmos, was caught up into heaven. There, he heard the voice of God, saw the ultimate Throne and a bit of the administration of prayer activity in heaven – incense and thunder, thrones and authority, the prayers of the saints and heavenly elders with angelic activity (Rev. 1:4-5).

Perhaps you have a particular place that is holy to you in a similar way. Or a place where you once met God in a powerful way. It may be a beach, where you have walked countless times. There, the water rolls relentlessly onto the sand, as it has for millenniums, and one day you caught a glimpse of eternity. It may be a familiar place where God always seems close and all's right with the world – a mountain vista that has taken you close to the stars and seemingly closer to God, a home church or family cemetery, or even your own backyard and garden. Do you have a place where you go and feel especially close to God? Perhaps you can recall a place you remember as a source of spiritual awakening, where you felt particularly connected to God, and revisit the place. Here is what you may discover.

"What is significant about sacred places turns out not to be the places themselves," writes Thomas Bender in *Power of Place*. "Their power lies within their role in marshaling our inner resources and binding us to our beliefs."[47] While places can bind us to our beliefs, so can memory, a piece of music, a special story, a word spoken at just the right time – my guess is, if we think about it, most of us have experienced a 'thin place' in which we can remember God seeming very close and very real.

Not the Place – It Is the Person

"We're glad to be *in* the house of God today!" That expression is

---

47 Bender, Thomas. *The Power of Place.* Quoted by Frederic Brussat and Mary Ann Brussat, *Spiritual Literacy: Reading the Sacred in Everyday Life* (Simon and Schuster, 1998), 94.

often standard on Sunday mornings as congregations gather. There is usually a hardy and sincere 'amen.' In the truest sense, we probably should add, "and we are glad to *be* the house of God!"

In the Old Testament, the perennial emphasis was on holy *places*. The land of Israel is the 'holy land.' The tabernacle and temple had their 'holy and Most Holy *Place*.' The land of the Bible was decorated with altars and crowned with the holy city – Jerusalem. Where God had showed up – Bethel, Carmel, Mamre and more – men built altars to mark the place where He had revealed Himself. With the inauguration of the central altar of the tabernacle and then the temple, God sent fire from heaven that was to be perpetually maintained. *"A fire shall always be burning on the altar; it shall never go out."* (Lev. 6:13). Over the tabernacle by day, there was cloud, and by night a pillar of fire (Ex. 13:21-22; 40:38). The tablets, the word written on stone, was placed in tabernacle, inside the Ark of the Covenant. All of these things reinforced the idea of the holy *place*.

> O, to be known at the throne!
>
> – Samuel Chadwick, *The Path of Prayer.*

In the New Testament, the 'Word' that was with God, that was God, became flesh and dwelt, 'tabernacled,' among us, and we beheld the glory of God the Father. This is the incarnation – God in Christ, the Word poured into human flesh. In the Old Testament, the word from God was invested in a holy *place*. In the New Testament, the word was incarnated in a holy *person*. God found a perfect tabernacle in Christ.

> *In the beginning was the Word, and the Word was with God, and the Word was God. He was in the beginning with God. All things were made through him, and without him was not anything made that was made. In him was life, and the life was the light of men. And the light shines in the darkness, and the darkness did not comprehend it* (John 1:1-5).

And the Word became flesh and dwelt [tabernacle] among us, and we beheld His glory, the glory as of the only begotten of the Father, full of grace and truth (v. 14).

The glory of God that had been *over* the tabernacle was now abiding *in* Christ – the living tabernacle. And in the same way, the fire that hovered *over* the tabernacle, came to settle first, *over* the Spirit-energized church, the living temple of God (Acts 2:1-3). What happened at a *place* in the Old Testament now happened because of Christ, a *person* in the New Testament and, a result, to a *people* – His disciples.

In the New Testament, *people* are to be marked by God's presence. It is no longer about holy places, but about the holy person, Jesus, and his body, the church. It is about our being, like Him, a holy habitation of God's presence.

In the Old Testament, the *holy place* had been designed to keep the *people holy* by sacrifice, the symbolic action that involved repentance and consecration. In the New Testament, holy people are designed by living in a spirit of repentance and holiness before God, by their relationship with the holy person, Jesus, to transform unholy places into holy spaces – to be a consecrating, sanctifying influence on our world – salt and light.

Where God Deposits His Presence

In John 1:47, Jesus saw Nathanael, who would become one of his disciples, coming toward him. He proclaimed, *"Behold, an Israelite...with no deceit."* Nathanael was a pure man. Jesus revealed that he had had a vision of Nathanael. He had seen him in the Spirit before Philip had called him – *"under the fig tree, I saw you"* (v. 48). Nathanael exclaimed, *"Rabbi, you are the Son of God! You are the King of Israel!"* Before the other disciples believed, Nathanael knew Jesus was the Messiah – God incarnate. Jesus seemed amazed that such faith would come from his simple prophetic disclosure, *"Because I said to you, 'I saw you under the fig tree,' do you believe?"* (v. 50).

What follows is an amazing prophetic insight. Nathanael, Jesus declared, *"You will see greater things than these…you shall see heaven opened, and the angels of God ascending and descending upon the Son of Man"* (v. 50b-51). Jesus makes an amazing connection to the dream of Jacob and to the ladder on which angels were going and coming, from and to the earth.

> *Then he dreamed, and behold, a ladder was set up on the earth, and its top reached to heaven; and there the angels of God were ascending and descending on it. And behold, the Lord stood above it and said: "I am the Lord God of Abraham your father and the God of Isaac; the land on which you lie I will give to you and your descendants.* (Gen. 28:12-13).

We should gather up the content here. First, the ladder connects earth and heaven. Second, angels are freely ascending and descending, unhindered. Third, the Lord is at the head of this connecting stairway. Angels are present and active, but it is the God–man, heaven–earth connection that is important here, not merely angels. Fourth, the end of the experience is that people of the covenant, people of faith, *"…like the dust of the earth…[are] spread abroad to the west and to the east and to the north and to the south."* Finally, through these people of faith and their generations *"…all the families of the earth be blessed"* (28:12-14). This is more than a dream. This is prophetic destiny, unfulfilled in the Old Testament. Jesus is disclosing to Nathanael that what was only a dream of Jacob was about to become a reality. In the promise given to Jacob, God declared, *"Behold, I am with you and will keep you wherever you go, and will bring you back to this land. For I will not leave you until I have done what I have spoken to you"* (v. 15).

The purposes of God, what God 'has done,' and what 'he promises,' are dependent on His presence, *"I am with you and…will bring you…I will not leave you…"* So, divine Presence has about it divine purpose to which He is committed.

> *Jacob awoke from his sleep and said, "Surely the LORD IS IN THIS PLACE, AND I DID NOT KNOW IT." He was afraid and said, "How awesome is this place! This is none other than the house of God, and this is the gate of heaven" (v. 16).*

The name of that place, Bethel, Jacob called dreadful – not in a grotesque sense, but in the sense of holy awe, of the heavy spiritual content of the moment. Jacob respected the divine energy of the place, realizing that it was beyond anything merely human. Such energy is capable of life and death – awful and dreadful. Jacob exclaimed, *"…this is the gate of heaven,"* a portal, a place God made thin to reveal Himself. He called it Bethel – *Beth* (house) and *El* (God), 'the house of God.' Here, his grandfather, Abram, had consecrated the ground, building an altar. Jacob was suddenly in a place where the prayers of his grandfather, his own destiny, and the presence of God intersected. *"God is in this place, and I did not know it…"* Perhaps, he was exclaiming that he did not know the history of the place and that of his grandfather, a place marked by a previous encounter between God Abram. Perhaps he was confessing his awareness of God's Presence.

Jacob lacked spiritual sensitivity, as we often do. God was present, but he was blind to His glory. The place was alive spiritually. The ladder was only a metaphor for the idea of a thin place, an open heaven, where angels ascended and descended, and the presence of God was manifest. Here is the Bethel principle, "Wherever God, by a deposit of His presence [God is in this place], thereby establishes a house for Himself [Bethel], from that place, where heaven and earth, God and man, connect, angels are coming and going! All for the furtherance of God's purposes."

Stop for a moment and rehearse the power of this principle. This is about – a heaven-earth connection, angelic activity and ministry, the revelation of the Lord, our being a people of covenant, and the earth being blessed – this is prophetic destiny.

The argument is simple – God's house is not about a structure, but a relationship – and His evident Presence. Ultimately, it is not a place. Again, "Wherever God, by a deposit of His presence, thereby establishes a house for Himself" – stop! Where does God desire most to deposit His presence? Not in places, that is the Old Testament principle. Now, He is after people. *"We heard Him say, 'I will destroy this temple made with hands, and within three days I will build another made without hands."* (Mark 14:58).

Christ himself is the new living temple, *"...the Most High doesn't live in temples made by human hands"* (Acts 7:48, NLT). *" Do you not know that you are the temple of God and that the Spirit of God dwells in you?"* (1 Cor. 3:16).

From the time God breathed into Adam the breath of life, He has desired the human heart as His home. Redemption in Christ has now made it possible for God who, after the fall, dwelt *among* us as an accommodation to again live *in* us. In Christ, God reconciled the world to Himself (2 Cor. 5:19). Our new *place* is a *person*, *"in Christ"* (Eph. 1:3, 9), where we are made alive, raised up and seated with him (Eph. 2:5-6). By redemption, we *"are not in the flesh but in the Spirit, if indeed the Spirit of God dwells in you"* (Rom. 8:9). This is a

> In prayer, it is better to have heart without words, than words without heart. Prayer will make a man cease from sin, or sin entice a man to cease from prayer. The spirit of prayer is more precious than treasures of gold and silver. Pray often, for prayer is a shield to the soul, a sacrifice to God, and a scourge for Satan.
>
> ~ John Bunyan

mystery, *"Christ in you, the hope of glory"* (Col. 1:27). This Spirit, the Holy Spirit, who *"raised Jesus from the dead"* and now dwells in you and me, by redemption and regeneration, *"will also give life to your mortal bodies through his Spirit who dwells in you"* (Rom. 8:11). The energizing principle here is not merely eschatological – it is a present reality by which Christ, by the Spirit, dwells in our hearts, and roots and grounds us in love (Eph. 3:17). We are a living temple – each a lively stone, animated by the presence of God, collectively, a corporate temple. And from such people angels are coming and going!

"Hereafter you will see the heavens open and angels ascending and descending upon the Son of Man." Jesus is saying to Nathanael, hereafter, you will see angels ascending and descending on me! "I am the ladder! I am the gateway to heaven, the access to the Father." Here, in John, we are moved from the emphasis on *holy places* to *the holy person,* Jesus, who makes *holy people* who carry the *presence* of God everywhere, establishing invisible altars, sending into the atmosphere the incense of worship, to accomplish divine purpose.

Quickly, let's establish balance. While angelic attention may be cause for rejoicing, it pales in comparison to our clay bodies being a house for the Presence. That is huge. We are Bethel, we are the house of God, mobile, living, moving tabernacles. We carry an altar with us – both one of fire and the other of incense. We bind sacrifice and the sweetness of communion together.

In Matthew 18, with the disciples squabbling about the pecking order of the coming kingdom, Jesus borrows a child as an example. *"Unless you are <u>converted</u>, and become as little children, you will <u>by no means enter</u> into the kingdom of heaven"* (18:3). Here is the call to change – to enter the kingdom, you must have, by grace, the capacity for change. *"Whoever <u>humbles himself</u> as this little child, is the <u>greatest</u> in the kingdom of heaven…"* (v. 4). First, it is the childlike capacity for change that allows us to enter, and then it is the quality of childlike humility that determines how far we advance in the kingdom. Here is the Bethel principle again in a different form, *"...whoever receives one such little child in my name receives me"* (v. 5). In the embrace of the childlike follower of Christ, we embrace Christ. *"Take heed that you do not despise one of these little ones, for I say to you that in heaven their angels always see the face of My Father who is in heaven"* (v. 10). From this passage, the artist H. Zabateri, also known as Hans Zatzka, an Austrian, gave us the *The Guardian* (c. 1918), the quaint portrait of children crossing a dilapidated bridge with an unseen angel watching over them. The touching painting has been replicated by others in various forms. But, in truth, Jesus was not talking about children, but about believers – full grown adults, with childlike humility, *"...their angels...continually see the face of My father."* Here is Jacob's ladder. Here is Bethel – the house of God. Not a place, but a redeemed person – humble, growing and changing. From such people, angels are going and coming, back and forth, from heaven to earth. They attend us, because we attend God's presence and advance His purposes.

> Failing to pray reflects idolatry–a trust in substitutes for God.
> – Ben Jennings, *The Arena of Prayer.*

Immediately, in John 2, Jesus went into the temple – the ultimate holy *place.* John records here, at the beginning of his ministry, an episode in which he 'cleansed the temple,' overthrowing the tables of those who sold sacrificial animals at exorbitant prices and the tables of the money changers, who charged outrageous exchange rates. He weaved his own whip and drove them from the temple. There, he prophesied this own resurrection, *"Destroy this temple, and in three days I will raise it up...he spoke of the temple of his body"* (14-21). The holy person, Jesus, is pointing out, that holy places become corrupt.

And so again, the holy *place* is made holy by the holy *person,* Jesus. We need some temple cleansing in the nation, not by the disruptive throwing around of tables in the fellowship hall, but by the permeating power of holy people in prayer. Holy persons keep holy places holy. Not the other way around.

This theme continues in John 4 at Jacob's well in Samaria where Jesus meets a sinner woman. The disciples go to the nearby village for food. Jesus remains by the well, and that afternoon meets a discarded woman whose relational life is a wreck. At an hour when the well is usually abandoned, she comes for water to avoid contact with other villagers. There, she encounters Jesus, who breaks with racial tradition and asks her for a drink of water. *"Please give me a drink,"* he requests of her. She is mystified, surprised by his overture, his willingness to drink from her Samaritan dipper. *"How can you, a Jew, ask for a drink from me, a Samaritan woman?"* The request for water cast aside, she desires to know what kind of Jew would, by the standards of his peers, compromise himself by receiving water from her. With gentleness and humility, even vulnerability, Jesus empowers the woman. He provides the opportunity for her to be noble, to act in a compassionate manner. He makes no initial demand, simply a request, probing her own social sensitivity – will she, a Samaritan, with her own set of prejudices, be kind to him? Then he probes her potential spiritual hunger. *"If you knew the gift of God, and who it is who says to you, 'Give Me a drink,' you would have asked Him, and He would have given you living water."* It is a metaphor. He invites her into mystery, to taste water that is not mere H_2O. She answers in left-brain mode, *"Sir, You have nothing to draw with, and the well is deep. Where then do You get that living water?"* We are forever trapped by pragmatic Christianity, a rational approach to faith that strips the wonder away – and such faith is not faith at all. It always leads to argumentation, to contention. It is laced with pride, "Who are you to tell me what I need or don't need?" Rather than a healthy hunger for God paired with the humility necessary to learn and grow, we harden – "*Are You greater than our father Jacob, who gave us the well, and drank from it himself, as well as his sons and his livestock?*" Translated, "You have no bucket. You don't have what it takes to help me!" Here is a tired, weary Jew, without a bucket or a dipper, asking water of her, and yet offering to take her to a deeper place spiritually. God, here, is in disguise, hidden.

One thing we must ever learn in the prayer journey is that the most unlikely people may, at points, be our most powerful mentors. The 'child' leads. It is not often the mighty or noble, who know how to enter a prayer closet and prevail in intercessory prayer, who ride the magic carpet of prayer around the world, who time-travel – interfering with future events, claiming and interceding for the purposes of God to break into our time-space world – it is the humble one in whom God is hidden.

> Our true character comes out in the way we pray.
> –Oswald Chambers

Jesus promised her, and us, "*...a fountain of water...springing up into everlasting life.*" Her response is a humble, "*Sir, give me this water...*" Yet, she is still thinking in the old paradigm; notice her comment carefully, "*...so that I won't get thirsty or have to keep coming here to draw water.*" Jesus has just crossed the first hurdle, evoking humility, touching the hunger inside her. Now comes the second hurdle, honesty and a hunger for holiness, a willingness to change, to be converted, "*Go, call your husband, and come here.*" It is as if he is conjecturing, "I'd love to talk to the two of you together. Because if I give you this water, it will change your home, change the relationship that you and he have." Indeed, the woman answered with a partial truth, "*I have no husband.*" Jesus is direct, "*You have well said, 'I have* *no husband,' for you have had five husbands, and the one whom you now have is not your husband; in that you spoke truly."*

The conversation shifts again, *"Sir,"* she says to him, *"I perceive that You are a prophet.* We have now moved to a third hurdle. The first was humility necessary to acknowledge need, desire and an inner thirst. The second was honesty, integrity, the openness to change. The water is worthless unless it produces a healthy soul, and that is tied to repentance and truthfulness. But there is soon a new roadblock – religion, tradition. *"Our ancestors..."*, the church I was raised in, my daddy and mother who taught me, they *"worshipped on this mountain."* Translated, "I go to church at...I have heard about what you teach, you *'...say that in Jerusalem is the place where one ought to worship.'"* That is, "You think we worship in the wrong place; you are going to try to get me to come to your place of worship!"

Jesus' response is stunning, *"...the hour is coming when you... will neither on this mountain, nor in Jerusalem, worship the Father."* It is not about the *place! – "...true worshipers will worship the Father in spirit and truth..."* Then Jesus says, shockingly, *"the Father is seeking such to worship Him."* Looking. Searching. All over your city – at wells and water fountains, at bus stops and taxi stands, at intersections and underpasses, in banks and garages, high-rises and apartment flats, on playgrounds and in office complexes, God is looking for worshippers! People who will simply pray, invite the Presence, celebrate Him.

"I know that Messiah is coming" – she seems now to understand this is not about a place, it is about a person, *"When He comes, He will tell us all things."* Understanding she correctly believes, comes in our relationship with the Messiah. *"Jesus said to her, 'I who speak to you am He.'"* An incredible thing happens as the disciples return and recognize the woman as a Samaritan. They are astonished that Jesus is engaged in a conversation with her. Suddenly, the woman rushes

into town, telling the people, *"Come, see a man who told me every-thing...Could he possibly be the Messiah?"* Here, the discredited one becomes the witness. God's ways are strange. The Samaritan sinner woman becomes an evangelist, and the people of the city follow her back to the well to meet Jesus. The disciples brought back snacks; she brought back the city! You say, 'In four more months, the harvest will begin?' Look," Jesus is now pointing to the crowd coming from the city, *"Behold, I say to you, lift up your eyes and look at the fields, for they are already white for harvest!"* What does it take to wake up a city? – Maybe it is a single person convinced that Jesus is more than a mere man. It's not the place – it is the person. Which mountain do we worship at – Gerizim or Jerusalem? Neither. You worship "in spirit and in truth."

This theme continues. In John 5, Jesus was back in Jerusalem at the Sheep Pool. There, the porches around the pool were filled with sick folks. At this holy *place*, they were waiting on a miracle, the supernatural stirring of the water (v. 3). A legend persisted that at an unexpected moment, an unseen angel stirred the waters and the first one in was healed (v. 4). How often this happened or long it had been since the last stirring is not disclosed. There is no indication that the legend was true – but desperate people with little hope had put their faith in this 'holy place.' The man in the story had been at the pool for 38 years (v. 5). No miracle. Jesus walked through the labyrinth of crippled and diseased humans and came to this one man. *"Do you want to be made well?"* Jesus was probing his hunger. The crippled man dodged the question, *"Sir, I have no man to put me into the pool when the water is stirred up; but while I am coming, another steps down before me."* He rationalizes, "It is not my fault I am like I am," Jesus commands, *"Rise, take up your bed, and walk."* Immediately, he was healed – after 38 years. It was not the holy *place*, but the encounter with the holy *person*, Jesus.

Encounter Psalms

There are certain passages of Scripture that are especially helpful in transporting us to a special place in God. Actually, to an encounter not with a place, but with God Himself. The words and images of Psalm 27 point beyond a geographic location to a kind of thin place where humans and God meet in a glorious intimacy.

> *The Lord is my light and my salvation; whom shall I fear? The Lord is the stronghold of my life, of whom shall I be afraid? Come, my heart says, seek God's face. Your face O Lord do I seek, Do not hide your face from me. I believe that I shall see the goodness of the Lord in the land of the living.*

This is an *encounter* psalm, a meeting with God. It begins with an affirmation of God and proceeds to speak of conflict and persistence through that conflict. God's faithfulness in the past is the basis of a declaration of faith in His character. *"The Lord is my light!"* – and 'my salvation.' His whole hope is on God. This is the only place in the Bible in which God is referred to as 'my light' (See also, Psa. 11, 18, 23, 91, 93, 100, 118, 145). Despite the pending danger, the focus of the psalmist is not first on the *hand* of God for intervention or deliverance, but on the *face* of God. *"Do not hide your face from me,"* he pleads. Something has disrupted the relationship – and it is the restoration of the relationship that he longs for most. The Lord's face exudes light and an assurance of salvation. What an idea – the bright countenance of God! And with His face in view, fear is dispelled. *"Hear, O Lord, when I cry aloud, be gracious to me and answer me! Do not give me up to the will of my adversaries for false witnesses have risen against me, and they are breathing out violence."*

He asks for a 'hearing' in the courtroom of heaven. His plea is passionate, *"I cry aloud."* He is caught between real enemies with skin and lethal weapons, false witnesses that skew truth, a frontal assault that has grown deadly – but his plea is to *"see the face of God."*

Each day, most of us ask, or are asked by someone, "How's it going?" We usually answer without thinking. "Pretty good…not bad… great!" Often, we are only making sounds at one another, because we barely notice things unless our day is horribly disordered and out of the normal. One mother tucks her kids into bed at night and asks them, "Where did you meet God today?" Not surprisingly, they tell her – "Susie helped me…Billy fell down, and I got to go to the infirmary with him to cheer him up…There was a little rainbow in the water-sprayer on the playground, and I almost ran right through it. I could almost touch it." These moments may not sound spiritual to us but the children see God in the help of another, and in their helping another, in showing compassion and in little nature moments. We are often blind to such small God moments. This mother also tells her children where she encountered God that day as well – "I said a little prayer, and there was the thing I thought I had lost…I had a moment of so much joy and peace – and I know it was God…I ran into an old friend, and it was a divine appointment." The last thing these kids consider before drifting off to sleep is a God who regularly enters their world.

> Prayer can never be in excess.
> – Spurgeon

There is an old prayer that asks, "Where is my home? Is it the house where I live, the garden where I sit in summer, the country where I roam, or the church where I worship? The place I call home is where my heart is at rest. And my heart is most at rest when it turns to God in prayer. So wherever I pray is home."

Review Questions:

1. Make a list of places where you have felt especially close to God.

2. Discuss the idea of 'holy places' and 'holy persons,' especially the 'holy person – Jesus,' in light of the Old and New Testament. What is the 'Bethel' principle? What are its implications today?

3. What stands out to you in the encounter of Jesus with the Samaritan woman? What can we learn from his approach? Do you find God probing your thirst level?

4. Review Psalm 27 as an 'encounter psalm.' Look for other psalms which encourage an 'encounter' with God. Review the characteristics of encounter psalms.

5. In Matthew 18, there are two essentials that Jesus sets forward, first for entering the kingdom, and then for advancing in it. What are they? How are you doing with these two critical essentials?

10
CREATING INVISIBLE ALTARS

So we fix our eyes not on what is seen, but on what is unseen, since what is seen is temporary, but what is unseen is eternal. (2 Cor. 4:18, NIV)

In the Old Testament, the substantive was symbolic of something invisible. Those shadows of things to come, found their reality in Christ. Colossians 2:17 declares, *"For these rules are only shadows of the reality yet to come. And Christ himself is that reality"* (NIV). The NAS and the ESV say, *"… the substance belongs to Christ."* The KJV version, however, reads, *"…but the body is of Christ."* The GWT makes the obscure more plain, *"These are a shadow of the things to come, but the body [that casts the shadow] belongs to Christ."*

> The best way to fight against sin is to fight it on our knees.
>
> ~ Phillip Henry

What a fascinating idea – the tangible was only a shadow! The intangible, invisible Christ was nearby, unseen, undetected, casting the shadow over the altar, the sacrifices, the sanctification at the laver, the breaking of bread at the table, the lampstand with its fruit and fire, the golden altar, and, of course, the Ark of the Covenant. Indeed, over the whole tabernacle. Now, he *is* the tabernacle – the blood and the water, the bread and the oil, the incense and the mercy seat. All invisible. All intangible.

The paradigm is now inverted. In the Old Testament, we now know, the priest attended only a shadow. To them, of course, it was a physical altar. They were blind to the Presence, the invisible 'body' hovering over them, casting its shadow on the furniture of the tabernacle, its blood and basins, its fire and water, its life and death. All they could see was seen with physical eyes. The efficacy, even then, was not in the physical, but in the unseen spiritual. Now, Christ, by the miracle of the new birth and the indwelling Spirit, has been made 'real' to us, his followers. We now entertain God as presence. We welcome his invisible 'body' by the agency and ministry of the 'ghost,' the Holy Spirit. Jesus walks with us and talks with us. We feel, we sense, the certainty of God as Presence. Just as the Presence overshadowed physical objects and places then, it overshadows them and us now. Even if there is a visible altar, it is only a symbol. The power rises from the invisible 'body' of Christ hovering over that altar, that person, place or thing, by the ministry of the Holy Spirit.

This is not an easy concept to grasp – so let's look at the Old Testament imagery. There, a physical altar became the visible symbol of God's connection with man on the earth. God commanded these altars. The first command regarding an altar was in Exodus, *"Build for me an altar <u>made of earth</u>, and offer your sacrifices to me – your burnt offerings and peace offerings, your sheep and goats, and your cattle. Build my altar wherever I cause my name to be remembered, and I will come to you and bless you"* (Ex. 20:24, NLT). Here, an altar of stone, of earth was commanded. It was to be of uncut, natural stone. The use of a tool profaned it (Ex. 20:25). The ultimate altar was one of earth. In a sense, this is man! We are the altar upon which God wants to send fire. We are the dust into which He breathes and we live bearing His image. Having sinned, we are the altar on which He now wants to sprinkle blood (Heb. 9:19; 10:22). At the altar, sacrifice and the supernatural converge. Here, the name of the Lord is to be remembered, invoked in prayer, and honored, revered worshipfully. Here, at the altar, God establishes a gateway for blessing. The Hebrew word bless, *barak,* actually means knee, and thus, to kneel. To kneel, to pray, to create an altar – even an invisible one – is to position oneself to receive and mediate the blessing of God. The blessing never stops with us – we are blessed to bless. We are, in another sense, 'lively stones,' a living, corporate temple in which Christ, by the Spirit, dwells (1 Peter 2:5-9).

In the vision of Daniel, a plain stone destroyed the grand image of Nebuchadnezzar. It was, like the original command for the altar, an uncut, natural stone. It was not an object, not mere stone, but a living stone, a person, who toppled the corrupt kingdoms of this age (Dan. 9:34). That stone is Christ. Compared to gold and silver, the brass and even iron – that stone is of no value to the world. In truth, Jesus is the ultimate stone; the stone rejected by the builders that has become the chief cornerstone of the new living temple (Psa. 188:22; Mt. 21:42). And we, as noted before, are lively stones – both a temple and an altar.

The writer of Hebrews says, *"We have an altar..."* (Heb. 13:10). It is not the tabernacle altar. At that altar, under that system, the high priest used the blood of the sacrificial animal to atone for sins, and carried the carcass of the sin offering outside the camp. So, he makes the application, *"So also Jesus suffered and died outside the city gates to make his people holy by means of his own blood. So let us go out to him, outside the camp..."* (Heb. 13:12, NLT). For the believer, Christ is both the altar and the lamb on the altar – he was crucified, offered on a cross – thus, the cross, for the believer, became an altar; Christ is the sacrifice. Wherever we establish an altar, we establish it because of the cross, and, in effect, we establish in that place the cross – the invisible sacred place at which men can meet and be reconciled with God. As we pray, we establish invisible altars that invite God's intervening fire and his blessing. The crowing sacrifice at the altar was the peace offering – and that is the ultimate goal, 'the peace of God' in hearts and homes, and communities marked by peace (Phil. 4:7; Mt. 5:9; Acts 10:36; Rom. 14:17; I Tim. 2:2). Indeed, *"We have an altar...* " This is, of course, the reason we are to pray everywhere – establishing invisible altars and raising the cross of Christ that draws men to him. *"Therefore, let us offer through Jesus a continual sacrifice of praise to God, proclaiming our allegiance to his name"* – here is the fruit of the cross, the fiery love of our lives, continual praise. *"And don't forget to do good and to share with those in need. These are the sacrifices that please God"* (Heb. 13:16, NLT).

Notice the components again – Christ, the sacrifice, on the cross-altar; the blood that makes us holy; and the call to verbal adulation, our prayerful praise, our allegiance to his name. And yet, not the vertical without the horizontal – we also share with those in need. Here is our love of God and of others – here is the living altar. Here is a sacrifice to God and a servant-heart to those in need – here is the cross. Here is prayer that invokes His name, that reveres Him, and love that demonstrates the character of that name – this is being a living sacrifice. Ignatius said, "It is better for me to be a martyr than to be a monarch."[48]

The Early Altars

There is a history of altars in the Bible, the place where fallen man meets with God. In the Old Testament, the most common Hebrew word for altar is *mizbeach.*[49] Its meaning, slaughter place, is not very pretty. Our altars are decorated, adorned with flowers and candles, chancel vessels and table draping. But that does not change the original meaning or current intent. *Mizbeach* occurs 401 times in the Hebrew Bible. It is derived from *zabach,* meaning to slaughter for sacrifice. The altar, a consecrated place, made holy by its connection with heaven, and, also, by the blood of the

---

48 Brooks, Thomas (Kindle Locations 1508-1509).
49 Small, P. Douglas. *Principles of Worship: A Study of the Tabernacle of Moses* (Kannapolis, NC: Alive Publications, 2013), 91.

sacrifice. It implies life by death. It is the offer of freedom, paradoxically, with full surrender. It is substitutionary – one dies for the other.

From the very beginning, the altar it points to Christ. It is God who chooses to taste death to retain the relationship with sinful man – what an idea. So the altar, wherever it is established, is a beach-head of grace, an outpost of redemption.

The first altar is implicit. It had to be established by God Himself when He took the skins of the animals and gave them to Adam and Eve. In truth, the couple should have died, *"In the day you eat of it you shall surely die!"* (Gen. 2:17, ESV). Instead, a substitutionary sacrifice was offered. That the skin of the sacrificial animal was given to Adam and Eve means, drawing from later practices at the tabernacle, the sacrifice was not a sin offering, but a burnt offering. With the burnt offering, the priest could keep the hide of the animal, but that was not true with a sin offering (Lev. 4:11; 7:8). So, the sacrificial offering in the garden for Adam and Eve was not a sin offering, but a burnt offering – a burnt offering that counted as sin offering. It was prophetic, pointing to Christ. Likewise, the offering of Christ on the cross was in the category of a burnt offering. It was the offering of one who did not need to offer a sin offering. He was without sin, thus his total sacrifice was counted for us – and Adam and Eve – as a sin offering. Christ entered *once* into the holy place (Heb. 9:12). Every priest before him entered twice on the Day of Atonement, first for himself and his own sins, and then for the people. What happened in Genesis, though we are spared the details, was a sacrifice that prefigured that of Christ on the cross. And from that cross, the seamless robe of Christ – an allusion to the animal skins of the first sacrifice – was given to an unworthy sinner, a Roman soldier! (John 19:24). What a picture. *"God made him who had no sin to be sin for us, so that in him we might become the righteousness of God"* (2 Cor. 5:21, NIV). The NLT says, *"Christ, who never sinned"* became *"the offering for our sin, so that we could be made right with God through Christ."* In Ephesians 6:14, we are wrapped in righteousness like a breastplate. The first altar was redemptive.

There was a second implicit altar, where Cain and Abel sacrificed (Gen. 4:3-5). There, God exposed motives. Cain's inner heart was revealed and he refused the change demanded of him. The third altar, the first mentioned explicitly, was built by Noah (Gen. 8:2). It was an altar of consecration after global judgement and it effected a revered covenant with God. Abram built three altars (Gen. 12:7, 8; 13:18; 22:9). The first was built in the land of Moreh, *"The Lord appeared to Abram"* promising, *"I will give this land."* There, at Shechem, he built his first altar – the place of God's manifestation, His presence and His promise. Shechem means *shoulder* and Moreh means *teacher*, so the altar

> The prayer of the feeblest saint who lives in the Spirit and keeps right with God is a terror to Satan. The very powers of darkness are paralyzed by prayer; no spiritualistic séance can succeed in the presence of a humble praying saint. No wonder Satan tries to keep our minds fussy in active work till we cannot think in prayer.
>
> – Oswald Chambers

was a testimony that he had learned of God to rely, in the face of opposition and barrenness, on the strength of God's shoulder. At Bethel, he built his second altar, and there he called on the name of the Lord (Gen. 12:8). At Shechem, he was promised the land and called to rely on the strength of God's shoulder, but at Bethel, he appealed to the name of the LORD, Yahweh, and thus the 'I-AM-THAT-I-AM' God, the ever-present God which Jacob would experience in full force at the same location later.

Sometime later, with dependence on the strength of God, the revelation of the ineffable name of God – Yahweh, the Presence – the Lord then instructed Abram to walk the length and breadth of the land, and in this prayer-walking journey, he was symbolically subduing the land, marking it in some mysterious manner (Gen. 13:17). So, we build our altar and come to know the strength of God, and the name of God, and taste the presence of God – and we, too, prayer walk the land. And, in doing so, we bring the 'shadow' of His 'presence' over the land; we claim the land with invisible altars.

At Mamre, near Hebron, Abraham built yet another altar. There is no record of a sacrifice offered on the altars at either Shechem, Bethel or Hebron. These were altars of prayer that marked the land, and they recalled some encounter with God, some promise, but the final altar of Abraham on Mount Moriah would be an altar of sacrifice. There, God spared Isaac, the promised son, and the sacrifice that followed, prophetically, prefigured the crucifixion and the resurrection (Gen. 22:1-14). There on the mountain, Abraham and Isaac worshiped, and there, on the same mountain, God and His Son would worship two thousand years later. The testimony of Abraham was that God would raise Isaac from the dead (Heb. 11:19), and, of course, that is exactly what God the Father did, by the power of the Spirit, with His own Son. At Moriah, Abraham proved his reverence for God, and Isaac his trust of his father. Here, God revealed Himself as Jehovah-Jireh, the Lord who provides. Imagine this: What are the odds that, a thousand years later, David would purchase this very spot for use as an altar to stay the judgment of God against the city of Jerusalem and the nation? And again, as with Abraham, a blood-line would be drawn. And in another thousand years, Jesus would come to the same spot, the temple having been built there – and he would become the lamb, slain from the foundation of the earth, carried without the gate, a sacrifice of love to take away our sins.

In Abraham's sacrifice, the altar and cross converge. At Beer-sheba, the Lord appeared to Isaac, dispelling his fear and renewing the promise made to his father, and there Isaac built his altar (Gen. 26:24-25), and called on the name of the Lord. Jacob, by the angel of the Lord in a dream, was directed to *"return unto the land of thy kindred"* (Gen. 31:13). He purchased a field near Shechem, where his father had built an altar, and he built one there, calling it *El Elohe Israel* (Gen. 33:20), the Mighty God of Israel. God directed him to *"Arise, go up to Bethel, and dwell there: and make an altar to God..."* (Gen. 35:1). There, he built the altar God commanded, and called the place *El-bethel*, God of the House of God.

The One Altar

When the tabernacle was constructed, it contained two altars — one for blood sacrifices, and the other, the golden altar, burned incense twice daily. At the time of the twice-daily offering of consecration on the brass altar, the golden altar smoked with incense. The altars became one. The brass altar was referred to as the altar of burnt offering, the brazen altar (Ex. 39:39; 1 Kings 8:64). It was also called the altar of God (Psa. 43:4) and the altar of the Lord (Mal. 2:13). The same pattern was followed in the temple — one altar, in two forms or shapes, brass and golden — and by these altars, the twelve tribes were united with God.

Now, we are united at the one altar in heaven (Hebrews 8, 9). We worship in heaven's tabernacle. One altar was the standard of the law for the unity of the nation. Ellicott reminds us, "A plurality of altars was the badge of idolatry."[50] The righteous were not the only ones who built altars. The unrighteous, then and now, build them as well. Alternative altars by pagans meant alternative faith options, a

---

50 *Ellicott's Commentary for English Readers.* See also, *History of Balaam and His Prophecies*, 392. biblehub.com/commentaries/numbers/23-1.htm.

plurality of gods and multiple choices from those gods – offer your sacrifices and pick the answer or outcome from the most favorable god. It was and is a system of spiritual manipulation and self-delusion.

In Numbers 23:1, 14, 29, there is a colorful story of Balak, the king of Moab, who wanted to curse Israel. He hired a false prophet named Balaam to speak the curse. A strange turn of events occurred. Balaam, on his way to fulfill the mission, encountered an angel blocking his path, but he was blind to the presence of the supernatural being. His donkey, more spiritually perceptive than the prophet, could see the angel and as a result, balked and resisted moving forward. In the passage, the donkey becomes the prophet, the interpreter of the spiritual dynamic, more discerning than the man, and speaks to Balaam, warning him. Still, he persisted. Balaam then instructed Balak the king to have seven altars built. The number seven was significant in pagan circles, as it is in Biblical literature. Some say it corresponded to the number of known planets at that time in history and was an important number to pagan astrologers.[51] The sacrifices and prayers were, however, at least superficially, directed to the God of Israel (Num. 23:4) but Balaam appears to mix pagan practices into the equation. Baal was the patron deity of Moab.[52] Balaam's curse was miraculously turned to a blessing (Num. 23:1-10; 23:11-21, 27-30). There is a note of hope here. God is Lord of even pagan worship sites, and of prophets who are false. His will cannot be circumvented.

In Greek, the common word for altar is *thusiastérion,* the meeting place between God and the true worshiper. The word occurs in the New Testament 24 times. It is the 'place' of consecration, where the Lord meets and communes with His people, any sincere believer.

---

51 *Barnes' Notes on the Bible.* biblehub.com/commentaries/numbers/23-1.htm.
52 *Jamieson-Fausset-Brown Bible Commentary.* biblehub.com/commentaries/numbers/23-1.htm.

In a sense, then, the altar is the invisible space, consecrated because of a heaven–earth connection. Somehow, an invisible sacred altar is formed potentially anywhere a believer hears from God and acts in obedience. The Greek word here is from *thusia* and *térion,* and it means

> Incense offers no fragrance without fire – and ascending sweet smoke. No fire: no fragrance.

sacrifice. Properly, it is a sacrifice prescribed by God and accepted by Him, when offered on His terms. Let's make this practical – it may be that when God prescribes an action, calls for some obedience, and we prayerfully obey, submitting, yielding, aligning with heaven, we are moving with Him, we become the 'shadow.' And, somehow, we make that space – that person, place or thing – sacred. An act of consecration takes place. In the very least, we by obedience lay claim to what Christ died for.

The altar is a consecrated place or space, and, conversely, the altar consecrates space and place, as well as people. Think of the altar, and prayer, as a way of marking a place or a person with a spiritual marker that only heaven can see. The New Testament writers see the cross as the king of altars.

It is at the altar, the cross, in which we are made like Christ – and we pray with such transformation in view. Pachomius was a soldier under Emperor Constantine. His army ran out of supplies and was on the brink of starvation when they happened upon a city full of Christians. Generously and graciously, the people in the city responded to the needs of the troop of soldiers, without threat or coercion. Pachomius was stunned by their free and abundant charity. He probed their nature, their motives, and discovered that they were called Christians. Their goal was to harm or hurt none, but to do good to all. In effect, they lived out of the presence of God (prayer), loving and caring for others and responding to the inquiries of such men as Pachomius and his band of soldiers, and sharing Christ. Pachomius threw away his weapons of warfare and became a follower of Jesus Christ and, eventually, a saint.[53]

Review Questions:

1. So, the tangible is a shadow, and the intangible is the substantive – discuss this idea. Why do we, called to live 'the invisible,' keep reverting to the tangible, substantive?

2. What about the idea that 'we' are the ultimate altar? Is this what is meant by the image of our hearts as an altar?

3. Many altars – one altar. Do you think of prayer as being out of the altar of heaven? Is this the idea most believers have? What are the implications of one altar and one high priest?

4. Did you grasp the impact of the first sacrifice as our offering of consecration – counted as a sin offering? Its relationship to the offering of Christ? The skin of the first sacrifice and the seamless robe of Christ – one in the same (symbolically)?

5. Review the altars of Abraham. Think, where might God want you to build an invisible altar?

---

53 Brooks, Thomas (Kindle Locations 1197-1201).

11

THE POWER OF INCENSE: PERFUMING THE TOWN

They call it 'Nonlethal Weapons Development.' The idea is to develop a next generation 'stink bomb' that can be deployed to encourage large numbers of people *to voluntarily leave* a building – or a city! It is a project of cognitive psychologists and odor experts at the Monell Chemical Senses Center in Philadelphia, all in the name of national security, funded by the Department of Defense. The CIA, the FBI, the Army and local law enforcement agencies see the potential of *an odor weapon* for use with crowd control and even in warfare. "Odor deterrence works! People don't hang out around dumpsters," they assert.

Animals mark their territories as a deterrent to intruders – and similar technologies are already in use by some companies, even here in the USA. In certain places and conditions, at certain temperatures, some smells are barely detectable to humans, but they discourage animal predators that have a more acute capacity for odor differentiation. The human olfactory system detects *changes* in odors more than it monitors those same smells. For example, the senses stir at the smell of frying bacon, but if the bacon is out all day, the olfactory system adjusts to its presence and ignores it. It takes about 15 minutes to adjust to a new odor – even a disgusting one – and then to be reasonably acclimatized to it. There is another problem – a bad odor in North America is not universally a bad odor elsewhere. As it turns out, odor preferences vary from culture to culture. However, one odor universally disdained is sulfur, the smell of decomposition and decay. Well, actually two odors are universally disdained, the other being the repugnant smell of 'Bathroom Malodor,' the standard reek against which commercial companies test their bathroom air fresheners. These two odors top the list of smells avoided.[54]

A recent article in *Parade* magazine, "What Your Nose Knows," revealed some interesting facts about our five senses, in particular, our sense of hearing. According to the article, at birth, our ears are pristine organs, capable of discerning among more than 300,000 sounds, but after years of exposure to loud noises, the hair cells on the cochlea in the inner ear flatten, becoming less sensitive. This constant bath of noise affects everything from our concentration to our health. But while our sense of hearing declines, we are born with an underdeveloped sense of smell.[55] Humans have about a thousand olfactory receptor genes, but 60 percent are not functional – we do not have an acutely developed sense of smell.[56] Animals do – they use their sense of smell to detect food and avoid predators; it is a survival mechanism for them. A dog's sense of smell is 10,000 to 100,000 times more sensitive, compared to humans. James Walker, former director of the Sensory Research Institute at Florida State University, says, "Suppose it is only 10,000 times better": here is what that means by comparison. If smell was comparable to vision, what a human could see a third of a mile away, a dog could see 3,000 miles away just as clearly. They detect odors in parts per trillion.[57] That is

---

54 Kahn, Jennifer. "Aroma Therapy: in the Military, It's Known as 'Nonlethal Weapons Development'" (Published 4:00 am, Tuesday, May 22, 2001). www.sfgate.com/news/article/Aroma-Therapy-In-The-Military-It-s-Known-As-2919298.php.

55 Chambers, Sandra (2014-10-07). *Lord, It's Boring in My Prayer Closet: How to Revitalize Your Prayer Life* (Kindle Location 4).

56 Schmeisser, Elmar, Kimberly A. Pollard, and Tomasz Letowski, "Olfaction Warfare: Odor as Sword and Shield" (ARL-Army Research Laboratory; SR-0258, March 2013), 3. www.arl.army.mil/arlreports/2013/ARL-SR-0258.pdf

57 Tyson, Peter. "A Dogs' Dazzling Sense of Smell" (NOVA Science Now; 10.04.12); www.pbs.org/wgbh/nova/nature/dogs-sense-of-smell.html

a powerful sense of smell. Mosquitoes also find us through smell. Plants emit smells and attract pollinators like bees and butterflies. Carnivorous plants use floral-like scents to lure their prey. Some damaged plants release odorous chemicals that attract predators, which feed on herbivores and, in turn, spare the plant. Skunks release a powerful and unforgettable odor when they are disturbed or frightened. Some animals have scent packets that, when injured or ruptured by a predator, send a scent signal, a kind of distress call or alarm warning to their social kin group. Animals navigate by their sense of smell as well. They determine trails, a preferable habitat, spawning areas by smell. Friends and foes are known by the sense of smell.[58]

The perfume industry manufactures more than a thousand distinct fragrances – at the tune of $25 billion annually.[59] To enhance the movie experience, that industry is now experimenting with subtle scent release mechanisms timed to the movie, either in the seats of movie goers or released from the ceiling.[60] By 2020, inventors predict that televisions will be equipped with an odor emitting capability for a fuller viewer sensory experience. Who would really want such an enhancement?

> Prayer itself is an art which only the Holy Ghost can teach us. He is the giver of all prayer. Pray for prayer. Pray till you can pray.
>
> ~ Charles Spurgeon

In ancient warfare, around 2000 B.C., Indian soldiers in the Far East were already using toxic fumes on the battlefield. Chinese writings also indicate the use of hundreds of recipes for poisonous or irritating smokes as a battlefield tactic, as early as the seventh century

---

58 Ibid, 4-7.
59 Ibid, 15.
60 Ibid, 16.

B.C., including a deadly use of arsenic called "soul-hunting fog," dispersing lime into the air.[61] Gas bombs were common by A.D. 1000, with a sulfur and nitrate base. Some of these weapons were laced with poisons that triggered heart attacks or asphyxiated their victims. In the Civil War, the North considered using shells that would explode over the Confederate trenches creating a chlorine cloud that disabled and made overcoming their enemy easier and less deadly, the battles more decisive, more quickly. Confederates considered chloroform. Compounds of sulfuric acid with hydrochloric or muriatic acid were also considered to form dense toxic clouds to disable the enemy with coughing and sneezing spells, teary eyes, that, in part, obscured the advances of the enemy.[62]

The Odor of Prayer

Forgive this excursion, except to note that prayer is understood in Scripture as an odor! As a cloud of pungent smoke – incense. Like many odors, we certainly don't have the developed capacity to smell *prayer*. Nor can we see it. Heaven, however, views our prayers, our worship, as fragrant, smoky incense. Both altars of the tabernacle and the temple were smoky and aromatic.

The brass altar that stood in the courtyard of the tabernacle had a myriad of odors attached to it – the smell of a crackling fire (Lev. 3:5), the fragrance of roasting beef and lamb, along with grain offerings, bread (Lev. 2:2; 6:15). These were 'sweet smelling savors' unto the Lord (Lev. 1:9). There was also the smell of death, of blood, and, twice daily, of the burnt offering. The golden altar was also burned twice daily with coals from the brass altar, and on those coals incense was sprinkled, and when it touched the fire the temperature

61 Romano, James A. Jr. Brian J. Lukey, and Harry Salem, editors, *Chemical Warfare Agents Chemistry, Pharmacology, Toxicology, and Therapeutics* (Boca Raton, FL: CRC Press, 2008).

62 Ibid, 4-6.

change produced a pungent, sweet, smoky odor, not detected until the fire and the powder met. That fragrant smoke, the sweet smell of communion with God, characterized the holy place (Ex. 40:26-27; 30:7-8; 22-29).

Of course, we are dealing with a metaphor here. Nevertheless, pressing the metaphor, what if prayer released some kind of atmospheric change, an aroma attractive to God that invited His 'presence?' An aroma of a healthy spiritual life, of holiness, of purity and wholesomeness, of godliness? And what if that same fragrance was repelling to the demonic? What if, as in warfare technology, an incense bomb disabled the enemy – not killing him, but sending him fleeing? What if, pushing our metaphor, demons had the capacity to smell prayer – and they hated it; worse yet, they were allergic to it? Sickened by it? I understand this is only a metaphor – so, more plainly, what if, by the sheer volume of intercession, we could lift holy hands everywhere and send forth a bouquet to God that was at the same time a warning, a repellant, to the Evil One? If we could begin to imagine, even by means of this metaphor, how prayer could transform the atmosphere of our towns and cities, its inviting and repelling aspects, its native properties that escape our sensibilities, its potency that is far beyond our imagination – perhaps we would be more motivated to cloud the atmosphere daily with incense. To smell up the offices and complexes in which we work with incense, to be the odorizers of our neighborhood. What effect could a praying church have on its community? What impact could two to three Christians have, gathered in His name, praying at their workplace?

Throughout the Bible, we find the reference to aroma. The Bible says of the sacrifice of Noah, *"The LORD smelled the soothing aroma; and the LORD said to himself, 'I will never again curse the ground on account of man...'"* This was despite the recognition of God that man's heart was forever evil, but the sacrifice of Noah effected a halt to future judgment, *"I will never again curse the ground for man's sake"* (Gen. 8:21). This is powerful smoke!

Paul the apostle urges the Ephesians to *"...walk in love, just as Christ also loved you and gave himself up for us, an offering and a sacrifice to God as a fragrant aroma"* (5:2, NASV). So the metaphor is seen in both testaments. What Paul does is to tie the metaphor – a fragrant aroma – to Christ and to the cross. Paul may be drawing from Ezekiel, who had earlier tied the metaphor of fragrance to the regathering of Judah from exile. They would return having been changed. Their transformed lives, not merely their ceremonial acts, their sacrifices, would be a sweet aroma to God. *"As a soothing aroma I will accept you when I bring you out from the peoples and gather you from... where you are scattered; and I will prove Myself holy among you in the sight of the nations"* (20:41, NASV). Even after Judah had sinned and been taken into captivity in Babylon, God envisioned their return from the exile as a fragrant people, a soothing aroma, before Him and the nations! Hosea pictured Israel as a flower, the blossom and fragrance of a tender lily, the smell of a cedar, the fragrance of an oil producing an illusion to the anointing olive tree (Hosea 14:5-6).

Paul presses the analogy in his second letter to the Corinthians, *"But thanks be to God, who always leads us in triumph in Christ, and manifests through us the sweet aroma of the knowledge of him in every place"* – what an idea. We triumph in Christ, and a part of the victory life we live is noticeable as a fragrance, *"For we are a fragrance of Christ to God among those who are being saved and among those who are perishing..."* (2 Cor. 2:14-16, NASV). *"And who is adequate for these things?"* Indeed. This is beyond us – beyond our capacity and our understanding. To the Philippians, he suggested that their gifts – not gifts on a ceremonial altar, but their very tangible offering to assist in his work – was *"a fragrant aroma, an acceptable sacrifice, well-pleasing to God"* (4:18). Here, as in the Old Testament, as in the sacrifice of Christ, giving and prayer, acts of love and incense are conjoined.

The Tabernacle and Incense

Aaron shall burn on it sweet incense every morning; when he tends the lamps, he shall burn incense on it. And when Aaron lights the lamps at twilight, he shall burn incense on it, a perpetual incense before the Lord throughout your generations (Ex. 30:7-8).

Without some understanding of the tabernacle, it is difficult to see how this moment gathered up so many multiple images. In the tabernacle, there were two pieces of furniture in the courtyard – the brass altar and laver. The brass altar burned constantly with fire, and the brass laver was perpetually filled with water for ritual purity. No priest passed it without observing himself in its mirror and washing his hands and feet – patterns and habits, walk and works. At the brass altar, the blood represented justification, and at the brass laver, the water represented sanctification. In the holy place, there were three pieces of furniture. Proceeding from the courtyard, westward, to the right, on the north side, was a golden table, and to the left, on the south, was a golden lampstand. Immediately before the veil was a golden altar with a crown and four horns. Beyond the veil, which had the images of cherubim woven as one with the veil and finished on both sides, was the Ark of the Covenant, the chest with the covering of the mercy seat, one with two cherubim facing each other and looking toward mercy.

In the moments in which incense was burned, these all came together. Fire was taken from the altar of sacrifice. The priest passing the laver would be required to pause, to examine himself, so that he entered the holy place with clean hands. Once inside, the live coals would be placed on the golden altar. Incense, in powdered form, would be found on the table and sprinkled over the live coals. At the same time, the wicks of the lampstands would be trimmed, and they would be refilled with oil (stored on the table) and re-lit. And the prayer, represented by the incense that now filled the holy place, would be directed through the veil – a picture of the incarnation, of Christ – and to God who dwelt between the cherubim, on a seat called Mercy, the Ark of the Covenant. All of this would be done under a canopy, a wedding canopy, a prayer closet, literally, called the *mishkan*, the tabernacle.

The *mishkan*, strictly speaking, was a set of ten curtains, dominantly blue in color, but containing the colors blue, purple, and scarlet on a linen (white) foundation. Embroidered in the *mish-kan*, which would have also served as the ceiling of both the holy and Most Holy Place, were the faces of cherubim – as if watching the burning of the incense, observing and listening to the prayers. Here, all the power of the pieces of the furniture came together – fire from the altar of sacrifice, water and purity from the laver, incense stored on the table of showbread, light from the oil-burning lampstands, sweetness from the altar of incense – all directed to the God of the Most Holy Place. Prayer involves blood – the blood of Christ; water – the washing in the water of regeneration; bread – the table; oil – the ministry of the Holy Spirit. Good prayer gathers all of those elements and comes into the Presence. Washed in the blood, cleansed

> There is a marked absence of travail. There is much phrasing, but little pleading. Prayer has become a soliloquy instead of a passion. The powerlessness of the church needs no other explanation… To be prayerless is to be both passionless and powerless.
>
> ~Samuel Chadwick

by God's sanctifying grace, filled with the Spirit, fed by the bread of the table, with sweet fire, burning hearts, we pray.

In my book *Principles of Worship: A Study of the Tabernacle of Moses*, I write,

> Twice daily, the two altars came together. Fire – the fire that quenches sin – is taken in the form of live coals and blended with sweet incense (prayer) at the golden altar. Incense demands fire. There is no sweetness without it. The smoke of the incense fills the holy place. This represents the prayers of the saints, the sweetness of their prayerful dependence upon God, and the purity of their repentance and redemption. In this climactic moment, God is taking the incense of prayer and releasing its power back into the earth.
>
> The earth has rarely been touched with the fire of judgment from off this altar, but that day is coming. And when it comes, it will be as if the whole earth were standing at the foot of Sinai with the mountain on fire, hearing the blaring voice of the trumpet, smelling the smoke and feeling the mountain quake. This encounter with the awesome God is to remind the earth of who it is with whom they are dealing. This final judgment is a result of the prayer of the Church – "Thy kingdom come, thy will be done in earth as it is in heaven!"
>
> Only those who have made peace with God at that heavenly altar, by the gracious saving work of Christ the Lamb, will be exempt from the fiery judgment of this altar.[63]

This golden altar that burned twice daily, morning and evening, was made of a special mixture of spices which was stored on the table of showbread, a symbol of the Word of God, the place of feeding. Here again, we note prayer and bread, prayer and food for the soul, prayer and the Word, come together. The incense gave off a sweet fragrance, filling the holy place aromatically – as we should do as we pray, after we pray. That the time of the burning of the altar of incense occurred when the daily morning and evening burnt offerings were given at the brass altar is significant. Here is regulated prayer.

---

63 Small, P. Douglas. *Principles of Worship: A Study of the Tabernacle of Moses* (Kannapolis, NC: Alive Publications, 2013), 37-38.

Here, the two altars smoke together. The time of consecration is to also be a sweet time of communion with God. And sweet communion with God is impossible without consecration.

Three priests were involved in the ritual. One removed the fire pan and the ashes of the previous offering. A second placed another fire pan with fresh coals from the brass altar on the altar between the crown and horns. The third sprinkled the live coals with successive pinches of incense carried in the hollow of his left hand. The substance was highly volatile and capable of producing a thick smoke.[64] The prohibition declared: "*You shall not offer strange incense on it, or a burnt offering, or a grain offering; nor shall you pour a drink offering on it.*" (Ex. 30:9).

Only this incense, as prescribed, was acceptable. There was a precise recipe for the incense. No strange fire or strange incense was permitted. In fact, it was deadly. And it still is. The incense that was used on the golden altar was to be, "holy and pure," and dedicated totally to use at that altar. If anyone used this fragrance anywhere else, for any other purpose, they would be "*cut off*" (Ex. 30:34, 38). Nor could anyone make a duplicate of this incense for his own personal use (Ex. 30:37). Prayer can never be an utterly private or personal matter. The ingredients included three perfumes: stacte, onycha, and galbanum, mixed with frankincense. Here is sweetness multiplied.

- *Stacte:* This substance comes from the myrrh tree growing on the hills around Mount Gilead. When its bark was cut, the sap would flow out spontaneously, generously. The word means to "drop" or "distill." It was converted into a powder, and crushed fine.[65]

- *Onycha:* This substance came from a sweet-smelling shellfish that came from the depths of the Red Sea. It, too, was converted to powder. The smell was detected when this perfume was

---

64 Strong, *The Tabernacle of Israel*, 95.
65 Conner, 51.

burned. It was, therefore, a concealed fragrance, only detectable when exposed to fire. So, a part of our sweetness should emerge under fire.

- *Galbanum:* This substance came from the juice of a shrub in the high country of Syria. One would break the limbs or twigs of the shrub, or make an incision on the tree, and the juice would flow out through the night. It was a bitter gum resin used to drive away insects, a repellent. As the two ingredients above, this, too, was made into a powder.[66]

- *Frankincense:* A white gum drawn from the incision in a tree. It was pure, sweet and aromatic.[67] The trunk of the frankincense tree has a thin-peeling bark. The trees still grow in Africa, Southern Arabia and India. A cut into the trunk allowed the resin to ooze out. It dried on the tree and was then chipped off and separated from any bark.[68]

> The Church has not yet touched the fringe of the possibilities of intercessory prayer. Her largest victories will be witnessed when individual Christians everywhere come to recognize their priesthood unto God and day by day give themselves to prayer.
>
> - John R. Mott

Salt was added to the mixture as a seasoning and preservative, perhaps a catalyst.[69] Salt is used more for chemical purposes than in foods – it is catalytic. Worship, like incense, is a combination of that which flows *spontaneously* (Stacte); that which comes from the *depths* of our being (Onycha); that which is humble and *broken* (Galba-

---

66 Ibid, 51.

67 See: Spink, James F. *The Tabernacle in the Wilderness* (New York: Loizeaux Brothers, 1946), p. 79; also: Little, David. *The Tabernacle in the Wilderness.* (New York: Loizeaux Brothers, 1957), 37; DeWitt, 39.

68 Alexander, David and Pat. *Eerdman's Handbook to the Bible* (Grand Rapids, MI: Eerdman's, 1973), 100.

69 Conner, 51.

num); that which is *pure and sweet* (Frankincense)! And prayer, too, is catalytic. This is a composite picture of worship. At the golden altar, the analogy is clear. The sacrificial life gives off a fragrance that is pleasing to God. And catalytic things happen. The psalmist prayed, *"Let my prayer be set before You as incense. The lifting up of my hands as the evening sacrifice."* (Psa. 141:2).

The incense has fragrance only because it has contact with the fire. No fire, no fragrance. No passion, no pleasing aroma to God. Here again, the two altars – the brass altar and the golden altar – are brought together. Also two tabernacles, the tabernacles of David and Moses, are brought together. The lifting of hands at the tabernacle of David is said to symbolize the evening sacrifice of the tabernacle of Moses. The burnt offering, an offering of consecration, was presented on the brass altar at the beginning of the Jewish day at the tabernacle of Moses. The lifting of the hands at the tabernacle of David was a bloodless act of total consecration, meaning the same thing the burnt offering meant, yet it was offered on Mt. Zion. It was a substitute for the burnt offering. Even at the tabernacle of David, worship was still the giving of oneself sacrificially. And prayer at the tabernacle of David was like the sweet incense offered at the golden altar at the tabernacle of Moses. Prayer and worship are always more than ritual and recitation of words. Worshipful prayer involves sacrifice.

Burning Incense and Breaking Barrenness

Luke records Zechariah taking his turn as a priest, standing by the golden altar in the temple in Jerusalem, praying and burning incense. It was, of course, the time of daily prayer, and the people were outside praying. Both altars were smoking – the fragrance of the burnt offering, the sacrifice of consecration, was ascending before God. Simultaneously, in the holy place, the coals from the altar of consecration were placed on the golden altar and the powdered incense was sprinkled on the live coals, producing the fragrant, pungent smell of incense, filling the holy place. Suddenly, an angel appeared, standing at the right side of the altar of incense. Zechariah was startled, fearful. The angel spoke to him,

> But the angel said to him, "Do not be afraid, Zacharias, for your prayer is heard; and your wife Elizabeth will bear you a son, and you shall call his name John. And you will have joy and gladness, and many will rejoice at his birth. For he will be great in the sight of the Lord, and shall drink neither wine nor strong drink. He will also be filled with the Holy Spirit, even from his mother's womb. And he will turn many of the children of Israel to the Lord their God. He will also go before Him in the spirit and power of Elijah, 'to turn the hearts of the fathers to the children,' and the disobedient to the wisdom of the just, to make ready a people prepared for the Lord. (Luke 1:13-17).

This prophetic word came at the time of the burning of incense. An angel appeared with a message from God. The long season of the barrenness of Zechariah and Elizabeth was over – broken. The son to which Elizabeth gave birth would be a joy and delight, great in the sight of God. The name John means 'graced by God' or 'God is gracious.' He would preach a message of repentance and usher in a new age of grace. From birth, he walked in a special covenant with God, a form of the Nazarite vow. He was destined to spawn revival in Israel in the spirit and power of the prophet Elijah, turning the hearts of fathers to their children and preparing a people for the Lord (Luke 1:14-17). Zechariah was mystified, *"How shall I know this? For I am an old man, and my wife is well advanced in years"* (v. 18). The angel identified himself as none other than Gabriel, *"I am Gabriel, who stands in the presence of God, and was sent to speak to you and bring you these glad tidings."* In a bittersweet response, Gabriel disclosed, because you do not believe, *"...you will be mute and not able to speak until the day these things take place"* (v. 20). He was mute, lest he spoil the faith of Elizabeth and others. Outside, *"And the people waited for Zacharias, and marveled that he lingered so long in the temple. But when he came out, he could not speak to them; and they perceived that he had seen a vision in the temple, for he beckoned to them and remained speechless."* (v. 21-22). Elizabeth became pregnant and for five months remained in seclusion, exclaiming, *"Thus the Lord has dealt with me, in the days when He looked on me, to take away my reproach among people"* (v. 25). Miraculously, both chose the name John – and what a prophet he became.

So, what happens when we burn incense? At least on this occasion, when incense, when prayer, was offered, God spoke. He broke His silence. Angels were released. He broke the barrenness. He prepared a prophetic voice. He answered a prayer for one generation that readied a mighty work in the next. He joined the generations together, fathers and their children. He turned the hearts of fathers and the children. He raised up an instrument of grace. He filled with the Spirit.

The Bible says that the 24 elders in heaven, who sit on thrones around the throne of God, hold incense in their vials, incense that is a symbol of the prayers of the earthly saints – my prayers and yours as well, indeed, the prayers of thousands of generations. We are not instructed to pray to either saints or elders. So, how is it, then, that these elders are the custodians of our prayers? The only logical explanation is this – these are prayers that God has heard, to which He has said, "Yes! But not yet." These 'yes-but-not-yet' prayers are committed to these heavenly elders to hold for their appointed time. That these elders, robed in white, a symbol of righteousness, sit upon thrones and wear crowns reveals their kingly status and the kingly status God affords prayer. Prayers have a governing power about them (Rev. 4:4). They are potent, and, at times, they tap the omnipotence of God, and He moves in the cloud of incense.

The Bible indicates that at some point in time, perhaps times, the 'yes-but-not-yet' answered prayers will become 'now' moments. They will be mixed with fire from heaven's altar, incense – the prayers of the saints – and divine fire, the power of the heavenly altar, the power of prayer, will be released into the earth. John describes the scene in heaven. Seven angels stand before the throne with trumpets prepared to sound. An angel with a golden censer stands at the golden altar in heaven, the 'real' altar, the one that corresponds to the 'shadow' altar on the earth. At this shadow, Zechariah stood in the narrative of Luke. When we pray, heaven's altar smokes. We stand at our altars, but they are only a shadow of the 'real' altar – the one we aspire to. The angel was given much in-

> The value of a daily habit of withdrawal and hallowed seclusion is beyond exaggeration.
> –Samuel Chadwick, *The Path of Prayer.*

cense, the substance of *"the prayers of all God's people,"* and they were offered *"on the golden altar in front of the throne."* The smoke of incense, the prayers of the saints, are mingled with fire from the altar, hurled into the earth – and, suddenly, on the earth, there is a storm – thunder, rumblings, lightning, an earthquake; the planet trembles (Rev. 8:2-5). O, the power of prayer!

In this moment, history comes to the ultimate answer to prayer – the time of God's intervention to make the kingdoms of this world, the kingdom of God and Christ! The question we must ask is this: are their moments now, before this ultimate moment in the eschaton, when similar scenes might occur, when here and there, God determines to take the collective prayers of His people and mix them with holy, divine, heavenly fire – and release that power into the earth? Yes, we maintain. Such moments do happen. In some ways, we are always in a race to fill up the bowls of incense before the cup of iniquity reaches its brim. To implore God to send mercy, not the judgment we so often deserve.

Such prayer must be sincere. It must be earnest and genuine. One of the great hindrances is our attempt to pray, to burn sweet incense, with a foul heart. When the tabernacle had been raised and fresh fire from heaven was on its altar, the command was clear – the fire at the altar of sacrifice was to ever be burning. At this altar, sin and self died. At this altar, divisions were put away and reconciliation was celebrated. It was a place of blood and fire, of death and, yet, life. Only the coals of this altar were allowed in the holy place, and over them, the powdered contents of the special incense, symbolizing communion with God and intercession, were sprinkled. Without fire, the incense had no

> You may as soon find a living man that does not breathe, as a Christian that does not pray.
>
> ~ Matthew Henry

smell, no fragrance. And without the right fire, fire from the brass altar in the courtyard that called for the death of sin and the consecration of self, the end of division (the peace or fellowship offering) and a celebration of reconciliation, the incense of prayer brought judgement, not life.

Aaron's sons Nadab and Abihu, Leviticus 10:1 says, *"took their censers, put fire in them and added incense; and they offered unauthorized fire before the LORD, contrary to his command"* (NIV). There was a prescribed procedure that involved the fire of the one altar (brass altar of the courtyard), and the incense of the other (the golden altar of the holy place, between the table and the lampstand and before the veil). The place of prayer was prescribed. The source of the fire, even the ingredients of the incense, were regulated. Nadab and

Abihu threw off restraint. They wrote their own rules for worship. *"In this way, they disobeyed the LORD by burning before him the wrong kind of fire, different than he had commanded"* (NLT). The ESV called it *"unauthorized fire before the LORD."* The NASB and the KJV called it *"strange fire."* The tragic end of their prayer and worship is that they died! The odor of their incense, a symbol of prayer and worship, was triggered by the wrong kind of fire – one that did not consume sin or consecrate self or dissolve divisions in peace and humility. There is an attempt today to come to God with fervent and excited worship that is far too superficial and comfortable with sin. In the Old Testament, God covered sin, but in the new, He desires to wash it away. It is not merely a transaction of forgiveness that God seeks in our lives, but a transformation of righteousness. A transformation that produces a sweet aroma, that makes us and the gospel attractive.

A great deal is often made of the nudity of the Garden of Eden – it is hard for us to imagine such innocence. From the fall forward, and the time the skins of an animal were given to cover Adam and Eve, humans have struggled with their presented and concealed selves. A whole coaching industry has emerged to assist us in how we present ourselves – presentation enhancement – how one speaks and stands, postures and even chit-chats. "What-is-underneath-the-resume" is the question being asked by employers, elder and deacon search committees and even prospective marital partners.

Jehoiakim was the son of Josiah, and his father had been the last righteous king of Judah. Josiah had led a nation-wide renewal and revival effort in an attempt to save the nation; sadly, he failed to see reform in his own sons. When Jehoiakim died, his body, it was discovered, was covered with tattoos, superstitious markings, the proof and prints of his sorcery. The Scripture says he did detestable and wicked things (2 Chron. 36:8). Before the people, however, the depth of his connection with idolatry was hidden underneath his kingly robes, but God saw its signs on his body and the idolatry rooted in his heart.[70] His reign was cut short, and he was deported to Babylon, the land of idolatry, and there, he died.

Duplicity, hypocrisy, doesn't work out well in eternity.

Review Questions:

1. It is an unusual idea, isn't it – odor warfare! What do you think of this analogy? About 'smoking up a city' with fragrant prayer?

2. What do think the meaning of a life as a 'sweet-smelling' savor to God really represents?

3. Review the passage in Luke 1:14-17. Think about the passage as a template. Does it have any application to the life of the typical believer?

4. Elders in heaven, on thrones, symbolizing authority, are the custodians of unanswered, 'yes-but-not-yet' prayers – what does that mean? How does it move you to pray more or less?

5. In the chapter, we noted that humans have a greater capacity for smell than we utilize – our sense of smell is somehow underdeveloped. Are our sensitivities to prayer likewise underdeveloped?

---

70 Brooks, Thomas (Kindle Locations 2740-2744).

12

THE FIRST PRAYER ROOM:
BACK TO THE GARDEN

After all of creation – the sun, moon and stars, along with the grandeur of the little planet called earth – God engaged in one final act in creation. He created an orchard and a garden – here is God the gardener, God who likes to see things grow and produce fruit. However, growing *things* was not the primary purpose of the garden; it was intended to grow a *man and a woman*. Their creation had been the crowning act – Adam formed out of dust, but in God's image, alive by the very breath of God, and Eve built from Adam's side, out of his sleep, sharing that image.[71] Created in the image of God, do we carry the image of God with reverence and respect? In the time of Tiberius, it was a capital crime to carry the image of Augustus that had been imprinted on a ring or a coin into any sordid place – a crime![72]

The image of the emperor was above such habitations. Should we not carry the image of Christ with reverence as well? The exact phrase "...the fear of the Lord," occurs twenty-seven times in scripture, twice as often as the phrase "...the love of God" (12 times).[73] Actually, loving God we revere Him' and revering Him, we love Him.

After creation, Adam was placed in the garden that God had

---

71 Out of the side of the last Adam, Christ, also comes his bride, the church, possible only by his death on the tree; out of his sleep, his brief encounter with death, comes the triumph of the church, his bride partner, over sin and death, the promise of life out of his life. He has overcome to make us partakers in the tree of life.

72 Brooks, Thomas (Kindle Locations 1141-1149).

73 Small, P. Douglas (2015-03-17 00:00:00-04:00). *Fear of God and Prayer* (Kindle Locations 87-88). Kindle Edition.

planted, one prepared especially for the couple. This was His wedding gift to them. The garden was a place of beauty, as well as a place of nurture with all of its fruit trees. Here, there was shade, a brook, bees and birds, flowers and butterflies – it was utopia. The Hebrew term for garden, *gan,* is from *ganan.* It means an enclosure, a place that is covered or surrounded, perhaps even hidden. Secret gardens have a long history; some were enclosed with walls and secret entrances. By its name and design, it was a place *to be defended* and protected, and, perhaps, a place *of* protection and defense. Prayer is like that – if you protect your prayer life, your prayer life will protect you. As we noted earlier, the *chuppah* is a covering. The closet, too, is a secret place, and here, the garden is enclosed – all metaphors for privacy and protection. The greater connection of all these passages is to the '*secret place* of the Most High God,' the ultimate 'Most Holy Place' and, with that, the promises of protection that are found in that Psalm 91 passage, specifically, to those who 'dwell' under the shadow of the Almighty. In truth, the garden was essential to the growth and fruitfulness of Adam and Eve, and on that, the earth mission rested. And so it does today! Grow in the garden, guard your prayer life – and watch God open a door to the globe.

> Next to the wonder of seeing my Savior will be, I think, the wonder that I made so little use of the power of prayer.
>
> –D.L. Moody

There is an old hymn called *The Beautiful Garden of Prayer.*

> There's a garden where Jesus is waiting, a place that is wondrously fair;
> For it glows with the light of His presence, 'tis that beautiful garden of prayer.
> Oh, the beautiful garden, the garden of prayer, the beautiful garden of prayer,

> There my Savior awaits, and he opens the gates; O the beauti-
> ful garden of prayer.
> There's a garden where Jesus is waiting, and I go with my
> burden and care,
> Just to learn from His lips words of comfort, in the beautiful
> garden of prayer.

In this garden "where Jesus is waiting, he bids you to come meet him there; Just to bow, and receive a new blessing, in the beautiful garden of prayer."[74]

The Garden of Eden was no mere room, no closet, but an expansive, beautiful garden! Jesus, we noted earlier, had no house of his own with a closet for prayer; he sought the open spaces of nature where he prayed, and, of course, the garden – the garden of Gethsemane in Jerusalem. Those who love to walk and pray will find the idea of a prayer garden inviting. Prayer gardens may employ artful prayer symbols or stations – visual focus areas created as reminders for prayer. Stained glass windows in a church serve roughly the same purpose, telling the biblical story, the gospel in picture. Another model is a *prayer labyrinth.*

This Genesis passage, however, is more than a simple prayer garden. It is an ideological maze. There is the mystery of the trees – the prohibition against the knowing of evil, even if it appears balanced by good. That is an unthinkable proposition in our current world, where knowledge is enthroned as a god. There is the tantalizing promise of life, eternal life. There is the stream that flows from Eden, paradise, into the garden and, flowing out of it, enlarges to four rivers, one of which flows 1,900 miles. There is the garden, a place where man meets God, and, by inference, it is a kind of tabernacle or temple, a Most Holy Place. There are also missing pieces in this early Genesis narrative, things critical to spiritual health – specifically, the

---

74 Schroll, Eleanor A. "The Beautiful Garden of Prayer" (Lyrics: Public Domain, 1920). library.timelesstruths.org/music/The_Beautiful_Garden_of_Prayer/.

lack of gratitude and worship of God by Adam and Eve. There is the mysterious conversation in the prayer garden, not with God, but with the serpent. And there is the wonder of the grace of God after man's disobedience and deception. Let's unpack the principles.

The Garden and the Two Wonder Trees

The Lord planted this garden, created and *put* man in it.[75] The Hebrew idea of the garden is a hidden, covered place of rest. In a sense, we are back to the closet – a big closet – but there is also a connection to the *chuppah,* because this was Adam and Eve's private sphere. This is the ultimate 'prayer room,' a garden of intimacy with God. There is a phonetic play on *garden, way-yiṭ-ṭa',* and *put, way-yā-śem.* This linquistic rhyme seems to intentionally send man to the garden. It is where God wants him to be, where God positions him. Twice we are told, *God had planted* the *garden* – "*...there he put the man whom He had formed"* (2:8, 15). Between the two mentions of the planting of the garden and the putting man in it, we are reminded that the Lord made all kinds of trees grow in the garden, pretty trees, trees pleasing to the eyes, trees with aesthetic appeal, trees that flowered and grew fruit. In the middle of the garden were two special trees – one was the tree of life, the other, the tree of the knowledge of good and evil. There is flowing through the garden a river, and rivers out of it. Trees and rivers. Then, again, we are told, *"The Lord God took the man and put him in the Garden of Eden to tend [grow] and keep [guard] it"* (2:15). The placement of man in the garden seems to be tied to these *trees,* specifically, the two trees in the center of the garden, and to the *river.*

The trees offered either the fruit of life or the fruit of the knowledge of good, polluted with evil. The river that flowed through the garden reached beyond the garden, symbolically to the globe. These

75 *Planted* is Strong's #5193; and *put* is #7760.

things – the battle between life and death, good and evil, the pure and the profane – reveal what happens in the prayer garden, then and now. The *garden* affects the *globe* – there is gold down river, pearls and precious stones. The principle persists: Guard your garden and experience fruitfulness and influence beyond its boundaries. The orientation between life and death, the choice between good and evil, the decision to grasp or be given what God allots, thus, trust and faith, the potential to influence the globe – all are in the garden of prayer.

Man was to *grow the garden*, but, more to the point, this is where God intended to *grow man*. Here, he was to serve as *gardener* (to cultivate the garden) and as *guardian* (watchman). The whole garden was his stewardship, with special attention to the trees and the river. It was a place of pleasure – as prayer should be to us today – and yet also a place of peril. The heart of prayer is communion with God, involving the sheer pleasure of His presence, but the edge of prayer is intercession (watching, guarding). Here, Adam was called to watch – arguably, to pray as the intercessor for the earth. In the garden, he stood between God and the globe. His watchfulness protected not only the little garden plot, but also the planet; his failure at the task led to his enslavement. O, the power of the prayer garden. No place is more sacred, more important, to be guarded and defended with more fervor than one's garden, your secret place of prayer. There is a delight here, but also duty – and healthy prayer is found in the tension between the two.

Let's gather up the intersecting concepts here – the garden of prayer was a place of beauty, of wonder meant to inspire worship. It was a place of nurture, meant to feed. It was a place of rest, meant to refresh. Yet, to accomplish these delightful goals, the garden also had to be kept, guarded, cultivated, worked – just as prayer also has about it a dimension of duty. It was a walled and enclosed place, meant for privacy and protection, and yet requiring protection. It was a place of transparency and innocence, and yet a place of potential deception and infamy. God walked in and through the place, calling to Adam. He still walks through our prayer gardens, calling our names.

It was a place *through* which a *stream* flowed that watered the garden and, ultimately, the earth. It was a place *from which rivers* flowed and one of them led to gold, pearls and precious stones.[76] There were two wonder-working trees in the garden – one a 'tree of life' promising eternal life (Gen. 3:22-24), referred to by one commentator as the "sacrament of eternal life."[77] The other was the 'tree of the knowledge of good and evil' whose fruit corrupted moral discernment. The very appropriation of the fruit, the 'grasp' of it, was proof of the corruption of discernment in humankind. It constituted the successful planting in man's mind of doubt both in God's word and of faith in His character by the Evil One.

The garden's forbidden tree with its deadly fruit made personal discipline and restraint critical. Caution and self-control had to be cultivated. Like our own prayer life, it is the heart of paradise, but not without Pandora's box. The first couple was given dominion and authority over the *globe* itself, but the key to that authority, the door to their missional effectiveness at the global level, was through their success in the *garden*. Guard the *garden*, and, in that faithfulness,

---

76 The term *bdellium* is uncertain. The NIV translates the term as an aromatic resin. The NET as pearls. Most translations simply leave the term undefined. Jewish writers, who see the term as referencing a precious stone, which is consistent with the note about gold and onyx, believe *bdellium* to be a form of crystal or pearl. It is compared later to manna, implying a small, white material (Num. 11:7). The word onyx here is also in doubt, sometimes translated in the Septuagint as emerald. Source: *Gill's Exposition of the Entire Bible*. See: biblehub.com/genesis/2-12.htm.

77 *The Benson Commentary*, Genesis 3:22. biblehub.com/commentaries/genesis/3-22.htm. The *Cambridge Bible for Schools and Colleges* note on Genesis 22–24, "The Expulsion from the Garden," reads, "Immortality, obtained by disobedience and lived in sin, is not according to Jehovah's will."

they would touch the *globe*; lose the *garden*, and they would lose the dominion over the *globe*.

There can be little doubt that Satan's strategy from the very beginning was to disrupt this place of prayer, to pollute this holy space, to interject himself, to get man expelled from the one place so necessary for him to accomplish his global mission. This is still his tactic – to keep us out of our prayer garden due to its strategic role, or, when in it, to get us to listen more to his voice than the voice of God. The great challenge in prayer is not to talk to God, but to put ourself in a place where we can hear from Him – to silence all the voices crowding into the space, outer and inner noises.

The serpent still slithers into prayer tents, calling attention to the tree of the knowledge of good and evil, posing poisonous questions! All his questions are noisy interruptions, intended to distract us by the self-interested quest for knowledge over wisdom, seeking of answers to his distorted inquiries rather than a cultivated quest for life (tree of life). This poison tree is the question tree – and while neither questions nor knowledge are evil, narcissistic, self-interested inquiries never lead to healthy insight – *"Did God say? You shall not..."* The serpent puts the emphasis on the prohibition, the limitation in freedom, the 'boundary.' He does not say, "Looks like you have a wide selection of choices here"; rather, his question is, "Why can't you eat of *every* tree? Why does there have to be a boundary at all; why must you embrace restraint?"

At first, Eve did not take the bait. She countered, *"We may eat of the fruit of the trees of the garden,"* noting the wide range of liberty. Then she rightly added, *"But of the fruit of the tree which in the midst of the garden, God has said, 'You shall not eat'..."* When she defended the prerogative of bounded liberty, the serpent moved from a subtle suggestion, to a substantive lie. *"You will not surely die..."* the opposite will happen, *"...your eyes will be opened, and you will be like God, knowing...* " The first question, though subtle, was to instill doubt, but also to engage her in dialogue. She passed and failed. Intrigued, engaged, the serpent wasted no time in planting in her mind a denial of truth and an accusation against the character of God. She listened, she followed, she saw, she grasped, she tasted, she shared – she fell, and Adam was with her all the time, silent and prayerless.

While communion is the pleasure of prayer, watching (*shamar*, guarding) is the duty of prayer – the work of prayer, its vigilance, necessitating discernment and discrimination. Let's review a principle – in the first two encounters between God and man, God does all the talking! In Genesis 1:28, the first recorded engagement of God with man in the Biblical record, God *blesses*; and in Genesis 2:15-17, he establishes *boundaries*. The boundaries protect the blessing. It is this boundary that Adam had the charge of keeping, guarding, watching.

We typically see paradise as being free from work. On the contrary, in Genesis, we meet a blue-collar God, a working and creating God, and He creates a man to partner in His work. The great work is growing and guarding the garden. Guarding is a metaphor for prayer. Guarding is prayer as a duty, as a task, as labor. It is a form of intercession – and Adam was the intercessor God placed on the earth to stand between Him and all creation. The fall does not introduce man to labor, either with his hands (growing the garden) or from his heart (guarding it in prayer). That is not new. What changes is the nature of the work. It is now, in the natural, sweaty labor, painful and grinding work, a battle with thorns and weeds, coaching life from the cursed ground (3:17). The nature of prayer changes as well. It too is more laborious. It too, will become a struggle. It will be fraught with warfare. The fall requires that man meet God now at a bloody altar, a place of struggle and death. The loss of the blessing has consequences beyond the couple. It affects all of life.

The Tree of Life

The tree of life, *etz chayim*, is mentioned ten times in the Bible, three times in Genesis (2:9; 3:22, 24) and four in the wisdom literature of Proverbs.[78] It appears again in Revelation as a live promise to the overcoming church (2:7; 22:2, 14). Then the tree is seen again in the center of the new heavenly Jerusalem – paradise, lost, is regained. Here are the features of the first Garden: the golden streets correspond to the gold of Havilah; the gates of pearl to *bdellium;* precious stones, the onyx, to the foundation of New Jerusalem. In the new city, there is also a river and a tree of life (Rev. 21:21, 18-20; 22:1-3) loaded with fruit; moreover, God is in the midst and there is no more curse. We are back in the garden – now a city. Back to the blessing.

> The more we have of God's glory, the less shall we seek His gifts.
>
> *– The Kneeling Christian*

In Proverbs 3:18, the tree of life is a symbol of wisdom, *chokhmah* – and in Proverbs, wisdom is personified as a metaphor for God. To seek the tree of life then, is to seek God, and it is to seek to know 'Wisdom' – not good and evil, not self-interested knowledge. This, then, is our orientation – seek God. In Proverbs 13:12, *longing fulfilled* is the tree of life. This is the end of insatiable desire – God is enough. There is inner quiet, rest, and satisfaction in God. And, in 15:4, the tree of life is associated with healthy, life-giving speech. Out of the inner life comes healthy language. Traditional Judaism saw the Torah, the law, as this tree of life, promising wisdom. Torah scrolls are still wound on wooden rods and referred to as *atzei chayim*, the tree of life. The law, then, the revelation of God, the Word of God, is the fruit of the tree of life. To seek the

---

78 Although it is argued that in Proverbs, the focus is not on 'the' tree of life, but 'a' tree of life.

'tree of life' is to seek God's word, His voice, His wise counsel. In this sense, the Word of God is wisdom. It is God as Wisdom, and its application to our lives is life (John 6:63, 68), wholesome, life-giving speech, the deepest longings of our heart satisfied. Those who do His commandments (keep the boundaries, embrace discipline) have the right to the tree of life, and enter through the protective gates of new city (Rev. 22:14). In Proverbs 11:30, the metaphor is inverted; the righteous not only have access to the fruit of the tree of life, they bear fruit, *"The fruit of the righteous is a tree of life..."* Dangling from the branches of our lives is to be fruit, and in this passage, it is to result in the conversion of others, *"...he that winneth souls is wise."* True wisdom, lives lived by the Word of God, believers with wholesome, life-giving speech, results in the salvation of others, their invitation to the tree of life. Jesus equates the right to eat of the tree of life in the midst of the new paradise with the capacity to hear the voice of the Spirit (Rev. 2:7).

Watchman Nee said,

> The meaning of the tree of the knowledge of good and evil is man acting apart from God, man pursuing goodness according to his self-will, man hastily and impatiently seeking after the knowledge that God has not granted, and man pursuing progress by his own means rather than by trusting in God...acting alone and independently, outside of God.[79]

Nee continues, "As long as man seeks anything, does anything, or acts in any way by himself, he has sinned, regardless of whether the thing he seeks after or does is good or bad."[80] The tree of life was not something Adam was awarded if he passed the test of prohibition

---

79 Nee, Watchman. *Collected Works of Watchman Nee*, Set 1; Vol. 08) The Present Testimony, "The Meaning of the Tree Of The Knowledge Of Good And Evil And The Tree Of Life." www.ministrysamples.org/excerpts/THE-MEANING-OF-THE-TREE-OF-THE-KNOWLEDGE-OF-GOOD-AND-EVIL-AND-THE-TREE-OF-LIFE.HTML.

80 Ibid.

– the tree of life was not forbidden! Adam could have tasted its fruit at any point, but he chose instead to violate the boundary God had put in place, to pursue knowledge, not wisdom, specifically, knowledge apart from God's revelation, separate from God's disclosures, contrary to what God called good. In the phrase, the knowledge of 'good,' good is *towb*, meaning beautiful – pleasant to the sight, sweet to the taste, aromatic to the smell. All these appeal to the desires of the flesh. Building a prayer experience that is pleasing, satisfying, comfortable, is not the most effective course to take. Prayer, at least in part, involves struggle, pressing down the desires of the senses, longing for the very life of God, trusting the Word and wisdom of God, even if we still have questions.

The tree of life appears to not only represent immortal life, but also something more. Watchman Nee suggests that man was created and endowed with life, but there was life beyond that life – the taste of something man had yet to know, a higher level of life in God beyond his created life. This is a life that was not his originally; it is life on top of life, life that comes from deep trust and dependence of God rather than self-initiative and reliance. This was life outside of Adam and not merely the extension of the physical life endowed at creation. The fruit of the multitude of trees in the garden would have sustained his physical life; the tree of life was a metaphor for his spiritual life. It was the source not only of everlasting life (Gen. 3:22), but arguably of of eternal life – something deeper. When he fell, it was withdrawn, God not wanting to freeze man forever in the state of rebellion and sin.

The River in Eden

Eden is understood generally as paradise. However, the Garden of Eden was not Eden, but within Eden. God created paradise, Eden, and at its heart, He placed a garden for prayer, for nurture, for the care of man's spirit, soul and body. Somewhere in Eden was a spring, an underground river that surfaced there. The Bible says the stream went *"out of Eden to water the garden."* It did not originate in the garden, but flowed into and through it. When the stream, the river, left the garden, it formed four rivers. The spring gave birth to a river and the river to rivers – from the garden, the globe was watered. The multiplication, the transformation of a river to rivers took place in the garden.

The four rivers are named –the first, Pishon, compasses the whole land of Havilah, where, we are told, there was gold, good gold, with bdellium (some say pearls) and onyx (precious) stone. The second river is Gihon, the river that encircles Ethiopia. The third river is Hiddekel, which flowed to Assyria. The fourth is the river Euphrates (Gen. 2:11-14). The precise meaning of Pishon is not known. Some suggest it means to spread out, to disperse. It is also associated with the idea of springing up. Gihon, the second name, means 'bursting forth.' One meaning of Hiddekel is 'rapid,' perhaps inferring 'rapids,' a quick-flowing river. Euphrates is from a root that means to break forth and it also carries the idea of 'fruitfulness.' It is the largest and longest river of western Asia, stretching some 1,900 miles. With each river, there is a growing intensity intimated by their names. Water springs forth to spread out, to be dispersed, perhaps indicating a puddling before it flows (Pishon). Then there is a bursting forth, a bubbling, artesian-like dynamic, and the pool overflows (Gihon). It courses like rapids (Hiddekel), breaking forth and creating fruitfulness (Euphrates). Again, coursing into the garden is a stream, a river, and flowing

> The missionary leaves by taking ship or plane; the intercessor leaves by shutting the door of his closet.
>
> ~ Ivan French, *Principles and Practice of Prayer.*

out of it are rivers. Prayer does not produce the river – but when we pray, it flows to us and through us, with its effect and impact multiplying.

This is a metaphor, a spiritual word picture of the power of the garden of prayer. In our garden of prayer, there is, somewhere a river, *"...the streams whereof make glad the city of God, the holy place of the tabernacles of the most High"* (Psalm 46:4). The river (singular) waters the garden, and then the waters flowing through the garden, become streams (plural) that water the city that is to be, a city of God, marked by the tabernacles (plural), not the tabernacle singular, but plural – the *tabernacles*[81] of the most High God. It is the singular-plural of river-streams, and holy place-tabernacle(s) that makes the passage unique. Most translations ignore the plural. The metaphors multiply here, the river, the stream(s), the garden, the city of God, the Holy Place, the tabernacle(s), and the globe. Both streams and tabernacles are in a plural form. This is problematic, and probably why the passage is translated so differently. After the fall, to prevent idolatry,

---

81 The English Revised Version, Webster's Bible Translation, the World English Bible, Young's Literal Translation, the King James Version, the New American Standard Bible and a few others, translate tabernacle or tents, plural. YLT uses the terms *rivulets* and *"Thy holy place of the tabernacles of the Most High."* The NIV says, *"There is a river whose streams [plural] make glad the city of God, the holy place [singular] where the Most High dwells."* The NLT makes both the river singular, and translates tabernacles as *"the sacred home [singular] of the Most High."* The ESV does the same, *"a river whose streams make glad the city of God, the holy habitation of the Most High."* The Holman Christian Standard Bible makes *streams* plural, but *holy dwelling place* (tabernacles) singular. The ISV does the same, making *streams* plural and *the Holy Place,* singular. The NET does the same, but the language is more colorful, "The river's channels" – here is the idea, one river, flowing into, breaking up into many channels. The Darby Translation expresses both the singular and the plural, but together, *"a river the streams whereof... the sanctuary of the habitations of the Most High."* This is the idea in Psalm 48, though mistranslated and difficult to understand. It is the idea that Jesus seemed to be expressing - the one river flowing from the throne, the heavenly temple, into, through many human channels; the one tabernacle or temple in heaven feeding many tabernacles, mobile dwelling places, holy places – which are really holy people, upon which God's Presence settles, and through whom He manifest Himself.

there was to be only one altar, one tabernacle, one temple. This is the only place where tabernacles appears in the plural.

The NASB gets both the idea of the river(s) and the tabernacle(s) correct, *"There is a river whose <u>streams</u> make glad the city of God, The holy dwelling <u>places</u> of the Most High."* The KJV likewise refers to *streams* and *tabernacles*. The Jubilee Bible speaks of *"a river, the <u>streams</u> of which shall make glad the city of God, the sanctuary of the <u>tents</u> of the most High."* Now we approach the better meaning – the one river, the many human streams through which it flows; the one tabernacle, and the many tents of the most High, camped around it, all now themselves extensions, expressions of the tabernacle in heaven. Gill's Exposition of the Entire Bible gets it right,

> ...the holy place; being an holy temple to God, consisting of holy persons, such who are sanctified by the Spirit of God, and live holy lives and conversations: and of the tabernacles of the most High; being the dwelling places of God, Father, Son, and Spirit. All of which is a reason why the saints should not fear in the worst of times.[82]

The Psalm finds its fulfillment in the New Testament, out of the ministry of Jesus, himself the river and the tabernacle, and by whom we each become a tabernacle(s), our bodies the temple(s) of the Holy Spirit. And into us the river of his life flows, so that out of our bellies streams flow forth, watering a globe – all connected to the garden of prayer. All of us, clay dwelling places of God – are holy places, holy people, who carry 'gladness' into a city. The term river in Hebrew is *nāhar*, meaning a perennial stream, not a seasonal spring or river bed that is full then dry.

The garden was a kind of control point for the kingdom of God carried on the shoulders of the couple given a global mission, created in His image and entrusted with the gift of dominion. In the failure

---

82 *Gill's Exposition of the Entire Bible.* See the note, on Psalm 46:3 - http://biblehub.com/commentaries/psalms/46-4.htm.

to guard the garden of prayer, the mission failed. The Hebrew word *guard* could be translated *watch,* as it is in other places in the Old Testament. *Shamar (shaw-mar')*[83] shows up some 457 times in the Old Testament in various forms. It is a verb, an action. Watching may seem passive, but Adam's role was to be active. The definition is variously to watch, to keep, to guard, to protect, to observe, to give heed – to do what you are told, to have charge of, to be the warden to, to be a watchman, to wait for, to restrain. It can also mean to treasure or to protect a thing as a treasure. The term can also mean to keep a thing within the proper bounds. Some things they should have decided that they would not do! Finally, *shamar* can mean to perform a vow. Adam was under an obligation. The blessing, with the boundaries that followed, constituted a covenant with God. With blessing always comes responsibility.

When we enter our prayer garden, our closet, God expects us *to grow* and *guard* some things. To intercede, to watch, *shamar,* taking a position in the interest of God with regard to a person, a place or a thing. This is our prayerful posture. The first Adam failed to either grow or guard his garden, and he fell. The last Adam entered his garden, and there, the fallen kingdom of man was righted. The last Adam engaged in battle over another tree, the cross – and he prevailed. He tasted death and rose from the dead. And he opened another garden – a new garden of prayer. Into that garden we can now go – it is not a place, it is a relationship, a kind of portal. Paul

---

83 Sheets, Dutch. *Watchman Prayer* (Ventura, CA: Gospel Light, 2000), 26. There are three primary Hebrew words for watchman – *shamar,* referenced above; *natsar* and *tsaphah.* They have a defensive and offensive meaning, but the intent of defense is dominant. In the New Testament, there are two primary terms, *go-reuo* and *agrupneo,* usually carrying the connotation of protection. They have a more literal meaning: namely, to remain awake or to be sleepless. They are used of a sentry, a lookout, a night watchman whose job is to remain alert and sound a warning in the face of trouble (Luke 21:36; 1 Cor. 16:13; Eph. 6:18; 1 Peter 5:8).

said that he was *"caught up into paradise and heard inexpressible words, which it is not lawful for a man to utter"* (2 Cor. 12:4). To John, heaven was opened and he beheld the throne of God.

The Eden Tabernacle Connection

In a sense, the Garden of Eden was a sanctuary, a holy place. When Israel came out of Egypt, God wanted to dwell among them, in their midst, and He instructed them to create a place at the center of their camp for His 'Presence.' It was called the tabernacle. In one sense, it was the Garden of Eden, made mobile. It was the place Israel met with God, encountered His presence, and came to know His name. It was always oriented facing east, and entered in a westward direction. It has a tree – the lampstand was framed with a curved shaft and six branches, in the form of almond buds, blossoms and fruit. The veil, separating the holy place from the Most Holy Place, had embroidered in it cherubim with their images finished on both sides. As at Eden, they guarded this most sacred space where the Ark of the Covenant was located, where the 'Presence' dwelt. God, as at Eden, was present – and yet, because of sin, exiled.

On the Day of Atonement, the high priest entered the Most Holy Place with a basin of blood and circled around the Ark of the Covenant, being careful not to touch it. He positioned himself on its westward side and sprinkled blood eastward, onto the mercy seat. As he did so, he was oriented toward the east, facing the gathered tribes of Israel outside the gate of the tabernacle. He gazed between the cherubim and knew that past the cherubim-embroidered-veil and the *mascala*, the screen of the holy place, beyond the courtyard, were the gathered people, exiled from God's presence. In a sense, he had entered the forbidden garden, past the cherubim, back to the place of life.

From the restored temple, Ezekiel saw a river running out from the holy place and through the court, the waters rising and intensifying, as the rivers had done that flowed from the Garden of Eden. At first, the temple river was ankle deep, then knee deep, then waist deep, then chest deep – a swimmable, formidable river, not easily forded (Ez. 47:2-5). The river flowed east – to the desert and then to the sea. Wherever it flowed, its waters brought healing. *"Wherever the river goes, whatever it touches lives."* Fish are found here in abundance, and fishermen are seen catching fish in places no one has caught fish previously (Ez. 47:8-10). This is the force of the prayer garden, the sanctuary, the living temple, Christ, out of whom we live – a river flows and a harvest of souls follows. To the dying repentant thief on the cross, Jesus promised paradise – Eden. We can have it, too!

In Revelation, the river will flow out of the throne room in heaven, out of paradise, the new Eden, *"And he showed me a pure river of water of life, clear as crystal, proceeding from the throne of God and of the Lamb."* (Rev 22:1). Actually, it already flows from the throne room, into and through our garden of prayer. Jesus is the one river flowing into the garden of prayer, and we are the channels through which the one river becomes many rivers. This multiplication happens in and through us, God's cultivated garden. Listen to what Jesus said. *"He who believes in Me, as the Scripture has said, out of his heart will flow rivers of living water."* – this was a reference to the Spirit (John 7:38). God's presence is no longer exiled from man. God will 'tabernacle' in man; the river now flows into man, by the Spirit, and from man outward to the world! It is no longer about a place, but about the person, Christ, and the people who follow Him (John 7:38-39). *"But whoever drinks of the water that I shall give him will never thirst. But the water that I shall give him will become in him a fountain of water springing up into everlasting life."* (John 4:14).

Both the tree of life and the river are found in the New Jerusalem as they were in the Garden of Eden, *"And he showed me a pure[a] river of water of life, clear as crystal, proceeding from the throne of God and of the Lamb. In the middle of its street, and on either side of the river, was the tree of life, which bore twelve fruits, each tree yielding its fruit every month. The leaves of the tree were for the healing of the nations."* (Rev. 22:1-2). The river is pure, clear as crystal, and unpolluted.

It is somewhat fascinating that we move from a *garden* in Genesis to a *city* in Revelation. They are really one and the same. The metaphor has changed. There is a very important principle in the shift, apart from eschatological implications. The world has moved from being an agrarian culture to one centered in the city, urban cultures. This shift is taking place in rural areas in majority world cultures now, and it occurred in Western cultures a century or so ago. From a missional point of view, cities are strategic.

> He who will not pray until, on good grounds, he is sure that he has all right affections and graces, will go to hell before his prayer begins.
>
> ~ Samuel Prime, *The Power of Prayer*

Therefore, the shift in Biblical imagery is more than symbolic. It moves from the metaphor of the withdrawn garden of prayer to the bustling city with its thrones, its powers. The key to mission is, as in Isaiah, seeing 'the Throne' beyond the earthly thrones (Isa. 6). It is coming to see our hope as being in God alone. In the setting of a city in Revelation, John sees the Presence, God, as central there. This may be our challenge. The desert fathers withdrew to find the Presence in barren and solitary places, and they gave birth to the Monastery Movement with its extensive gardens of prayer. The question today is, how do we live in the city and, simultaneously, in the Presence? How do we live in a manner that honors the throne of God and the Lamb in the midst of a worldly system with its carnal, self-interested power plays? In tree-less cities, how do we live from the tree of life in deep, daily dependence on God? How do we facilitate the flow of the river through us into the city?

From Genesis to Revelation, cites are mentioned more than 1,200 times, and nations are mentioned some 600 times. Cain, who went out from the presence of the Lord, built the first city (Gen. 4:16-17). This was the beginning of chaos, cities built apart from God's presence. Such cities themselves become a wilderness, spiritually and morally barren, places of *tohu,* confusion (Isa. 24:10). So, man, created to live out of a garden, now lives in chaotic cities, often, apart from God's presence, indifferent to His throne, with polluted spiritual streams and a population still pulling fruit from the tree of the knowledge of good and evil. Our desire may be to escape such places, but instead, we must engage them, as God did Adam and Eve, even the serpent, following the fall. We, following the example of God, must walk through the disaster zone where people are hiding, ashamed, silent, refusing to answer, gripped with fear, seduced and terrorized by the serpent in some new form. As Christ walked the streets of cities in his day, prayer must be pushed to open spaces to touch broken people.

Throughout history, whoever controlled cities controlled nations. Cities lead nations; cities set trends. Paul's evangelism strategy was cities! E. M. Blaiklock, professor and historian, notes, "Lose the cities...and the country is also lost. Gain them, cleanse their hearts, make them fit to live in, and

> The Church is looking for better methods; God is looking for better men. The Holy Ghost does not flow through methods, but through men. He does not come on machinery, but on men. He does not anoint plans, but men...Men of prayer.
>
> - E. M. Bounds

much on a vast front is won."[84] So, the quest is not merely how to establish a prayer garden, but how to establish one in the middle of the chaotic city. How to push prayer to the public square after our own quiet times with God.

After the fall, Adam and Eve lost the privilege of walking and working in the garden. Since the pathway to global influence was by the stewardship of the garden, they became victims in a world they were to dominate and shape. So have we! Cherubim and a flaming sword guarded the garden entrance, protecting the tree of life and creating a barrier between God's presence and sinful man (Gen. 3:24). Their first son died in a bitter sibling rivalry, and their second son left home full of rage and independence – a mixture of good and evil, a reflection of the forbidden tree. When Cain took sin to its greatest level, he also *"went out from the presence of the LORD, and dwelt in the land of Nod, on the east of Eden"* (Gen. 4:16). East – it is to the east that men would later journey and find a "plain in the land of Shinar" (Babylon), and build a city and a tower, an astrological observatory, a place of idolatry, a place to make a name for themselves (11:2-4).

The great difference between Babel and Jerusalem hinges on the absence if God at Babel; and the presence of God in Jerusalem, The choice at Babel, was to ignore the true God at Jerusalem, they chose to create a temple, a holy space to honor him. Our cities are Babel – places of confusion; or they are found under the shadow of the New Jerusalem – a fortress of peace, depending on whether we grow and guard the place where God has put us. And whether or not we rely on the wisdom of God or knowledge polluted with evil.

The East, the land of Nod, which has the meaning of wandering, becomes the place of the rebellious sons (Cain), of those who construct their towers of Babel, their false, idolatrous worship cen-

---

84 Blaiklock, E. M. *The World of the New Testament* (Ark Publishing London, 1979).

ters. The East is a symbol of lostness, even rebellion. Notably, it is toward the east that the gateway to the tabernacle and the temple are oriented – the door was placed nearest those who were exiled, to be accessible, as it were, open, inviting, to the alienated.

Likewise, the river from Ezekiel's temple flowed outward from the holy place to the east; it must flow to such places again and reach the alienated, those wandering, the rebellious and the idolaters. For those who wander, we must pray. For those who have gone away from God's presence, wounded and uncertain, angry and disappointed, we must pray. To such people, God has issued an invitation to return to His garden of prayer. The new high priest, Jesus, gazes eastward, with his own blood on the mercy seat, waiting for the prodigals to come home, back to the garden!

Review Questions:

1. Is it possible, that in our quest for 'knowledge,' rather than wisdom/life, we are still tugging at the wrong tree in prayer?
2. Talk about the garden and the globe connection.
3. How do we distinguish between faith that appropriates by prayer and faith that grasps, without allowing God the privilege of giving?
4. Explore the link between the river flowing into the garden and the rivers flowing out of it. Also, between the rivers that flowed from Ezekiel's temple. And, finally, the words of Jesus, "Out of your bellies, shall flow rivers..."
5. How does the idea of the garden and the city relate? How do we establish a 'garden' in the midst of our cities that bring some level of change to the city?

APPENDIX 1

Examining the Conversation in the Genesis Narrative

In Genesis 1, God is speaking, declaratively, creating! And in verse 28, he blesses man and woman, and commissions them. At the end of Genesis 1, Adam speaks, naming the animals God has created. Rising from sleep, he makes his declaration regarding Eve. In Genesis 2, God speaks to man again, this time, setting boundaries. Surprising, the next voice, in Genesis 3, is that of the serpent. And the first dialogue is not between man and God, but between Eve and the Serpent. Only then, do we have a dialogue with God and Adam.

God speaks into creation.
God speaks, blessing man and woman.
> Man speaks, naming the animals.
> Man speaks, exclaiming prophetically his identification with woman.

God speaks to Adam, giving him charge to grow and guard the garden.
> > The Serpent speaks to Eve (Adam is with her).
> > Eve speaks to the Serpent.

God speaks – both Adam and Eve hear him, remain silent and hide.
God speaks to Adam – asking questions of him.
> Adam answers God, rationalizing, blaming Eve.

God speaks to Eve – asking questions of her.
> > Eve speaks to God – rationalizing, blaming the Serpent.

God speaks to the Serpent – asking nothing of him; declaring judgment, cursing him.
God speaks to the woman – detailing the consequences of her behavior.
God speaks to man – detailing the consequences of his behavior, cursing the ground.

Adam names Eve.

God covers their nakedness – and expels them from the garden.

Both Adam and Eve heard God walking in the garden and both hid. What follows is the first recorded *dialogue* between God and man, not mankind, but specifically, with Adam. This is prior to the judicial gathering of the three – Adam, Eve and the Serpent, in which God announces his decree. That is a courtroom scene. Prior to that moment, God acted as a missionary, as an evangelist, on a quest to find the fallen couple.

In their sinful condition, Adam and Eve both avoided the one encounter that could save. As if avoidance and hiding, not only from God, but one another, would make the situation go away – they are delusional, as we often are, avoiding prayer, the one context that can cure our souls. They wrongly imagined that they could remain in the garden, and perhaps avoid God, as if that erased the effects of the transgression at the tree. We too want to remain in the garden, and like the first couple, we also avoid prayer, so God pursues us. This is the grace of it all, that God comes looking for us, calling our name, wanting an encounter with man, even man the sinner, who He will meet with grace. What a God! What a privilege – prayer!

An old hymn says, prayer is the "Christian's native breath." Without it, we die.

And they heard the sound of the Lord God walking in the garden in the cool of the day, and the man and his wife hid themselves from the presence of the Lord God among the trees of the garden. But the Lord God called to the Adam (Genesis 3:8-9a, RSV).

Apparently, God manifested as a man, they heard the sound of his footsteps, walking in the garden.

It is remarkable, that in Genesis 1, God takes the initiative, blessing. In Genesis 2, God again takes the initiative, setting boundaries. And when the woman, with Adam looking on we should note emphatically, chooses a conversation with the serpent, and takes the forbidden fruit, and sin follows, God again takes the initiative – and comes walking through the garden, engaging man and woman in a conversation. It is the Lord who initiates, obviously, with a greater desire to engage man, than we have to engage him.

Prayer begins with God. He is the first speaker. His words are more important than our words. They are fraught with promise and the warning of certain peril, hope and hazard. They empower us, blessing us, and they set wise and healthy boundaries.

What is striking here is the mood of this exchange. This moment is the greatest disaster in the Bible. It is the tragedy that cast its shadow over the cross. It is the seedbed from which comes the necessary global judgment of the flood. It is the ideological foundation for Babel – the confusion of listening to voices other than God. It is the source of the spiritual pollution of idolatry on every high hill, the idols only a visible symbol of some dark spirit, and a pretense for self-determination. It is the root of every malevolent self-interested tyrant's kingdom ruled by self, exclusive of deference for God. From this moment comes sin and sickness, death and division, pain and suffering, the dance of life with death – all of it proceeds from this moment. This is 'the fall.' And it was the ultimate tumble – we seem to have no idea of how far we fell in Adam.

While there is no record of dialogue earlier, it is clear – Adam did not hide when God spoke with him in the first two chapters. He stood, with God observing, naming the animals. He expressed joy in the presentation of Eve. Both were comfortable before God, exposed, with no shame and nothing to hide. Now, after their moment at the tree, after the dialogue with the devil – the mood changes. They hide. They avoid. They must be engaged to engage God. Even then, dialogue is not easy, it comes only with the probing questions of God.

The questions are good questions – even for us. *"Where are you, [Adam]?"* (Gen. 3:9b, RSV); *"Who told you that you were naked?"* (Gen. 3:11a, RSV); and finally, *"Have you eaten from the tree of which*

I commanded you that you should not eat?" (Genesis 3:13a, RSV). God knows the answers to all the questions, he doesn't need information. So prayer is not informing God, it is necessary therapy for our own spiritual awareness. "Conscience," Thomas Brooks says, "is God's spy in the heart." Philo called it "the little tribunal of the soul ... [a witness] for or against a man. Conscience is a court of record, and whatever it sees it writes down; and conscience is always as quick in writing as the sinner can be in sinning." Brooks says, conscience "sits in the closet of your heart" and "makes a journal of all your secret ways and secret crimes ..." It knows the names and places, the secret wickedness that has been committed; and it never forgets until it reckons with God. Thomas Brooks asserts:

> Let a man sin in the most hidden seclusion... take all the ways he can to hide his sins, to cloak and cover his sin, as Adam did – yet conscience will so play the judge, that it will bring in the evidence, produce the law, urge the penalty, and pass the sentence of condemnation upon him.[85]

At the end of Job's season of personal pain and loss, of doubt and confusion, God summons him, and ask questions of him, "Stand up now and *'Gird up now thy loins like a man; for I will demand of thee, and answer thou me.'"* (Job 38:3, KJV). It is only when Job comes to a point of repentance, that God changes his situation (Job 42:6).

Where are you?

Have you ever been lost, only to call a friend, and have them ask you, "Where are you now?" You respond, "I don't know – I'm lost." They ask you to describe your surroundings and when you provide enough descriptors, they pinpoint your location. When you are lost, you can't get help from someone to find your way, until they know where you are and where you are headed. God always knows where we are, but He wants us to know as well. The first step is the recogni-

---

85 Brooks, Thomas (2013-09-06). *The Secret Key to Heaven: The Call to Closet Prayer* (Kindle Locations 2777-2785). Titus Books. Kindle Edition.

tion of lostness. The second is the humility that recognizes that help, beyond yourself, is necessary. Both of those are a work of the Spirit. Next is the call for help, that's prayer. With it, is the confession, "I lost my way!" and that is coupled with a desire, "Lord, I want to know the way to find you!"

Adam confessed, *"I heard you walking in the garden, so I hid. I was afraid because I was naked"* (Gen. 3:10, NIV). The ESV and NASB are more subtle, *"I heard the sound of you in the garden..."*, the NET, *"I heard you moving about in the orchard..."* The KJV and the ISV say, *"I heard thy voice..."* And Adam added, *"I was afraid because I was naked, so I hid"* (Holman). An inner fear now drives him. He is already a slave of painful, negative emotions – the toxic consequences of sin have come quickly. He is not only emotionally off balance, he is cognitively impaired, not acting in a rational manner. The evidence is not only that he is hiding, avoiding, but it is in what he hid – himself. He is out of touch with Eve, avoiding God, and he has attempted to hide himself, arguably, from himself. Sin divides. It cuts us off from God, from one another, and from a part of ourselves.

The first question focused on their location, their position. The second question of God to Adam has a deeper, implicit concern. It focuses on their condition. "Who told you that you were naked?" God presses Adam on what he has not disclosed – 'You are operating on knowledge you obtained from somewhere, someone, other than me – Who told you this? Why do you believe this information is accurate?' We should ask ourselves - What elements of our operating world view are drawn from somewhere, someone, other than God? The ability to discriminate between voices is critical to healthy prayer. Of course, the next question is the one Adam had most hoped to avoid, "Did you eat from the tree that I commanded you not to eat of?"

The first question probes the alienation – 'Where are you?' The answer reveals the effect of sin – fear and avoidance, vulnerability, covering up, the desire to conceal, but also, the subtle recognition that in doing so, we 'split' ourselves – 'I hid myself' – the psychological implications: hiding a part of us, from ourselves. The second question goes to influence, 'Who told you?' It implies Adam's great complicity – who are you covering for? What are you not telling me? Adam does not implicate the serpent, by silence, he protects the lowly creature. The third question is, "What have you done?" (Gen. 3:13a). Now God touches the act of disobedience.

Question One: Where do you think you are (your moral, more than physical location)? Question Two: What were you thinking (the source of your influence, who told you that, who have been talking with, who is now in your inner circle, under whose influence have you come)? Question Three: What have you done? The behavior rose from the thinking, out of false information, and that came from being in the wrong place, at the forbidden tree, where the couple should have never lingered.

First, orientation – where are you? Second, to mental state – what are you allowing into your thoughts? Third, to behavior – what are you doing? The coordinates of your position before God, in the earth, are at the intersection of your thinking and your behavior. Once God probes these points, he asks no more questions. Once he probes the disconnect, the thinking, the behavior – he acts with great grace. In fact, he is no longer prosecuting them, but defending, 'Here is how we are going to fix this!'

The absence of integrity before God did not alter their consequences. Adam blamed Eve, and she blamed the lowly neighbor who had wandered into their backyard. Ultimately, these feigned responses blamed God, "The woman 'You' gave me... The serpent you allowed to deceive me..." Ultimately, you find yourself more quickly, when you acknowledge sinful behavior and deceptive thinking. God is disappointed, but he will go through the nightmare with them, and obviously, with their children's, children's children. In the fashioning of coverings, he commits himself to participate in their pain, for these coverings are only temporary, the ultimate covering is the righteous, seamless robe of Christ.[86]

---

86 Stedman, Ray C. "The Beginning of Prayer", (Copyright © 2010 by Ray Stedman Ministries; PO Box 615; Mount Hermon, CA 95041; *Old Testament Series*, October 5, 1980), See: www.RayStedman.org.

APPENDIX 2

The Garden Labyrinth

The idea of a garden labyrinth used for prayer is controversial in some circles and rejected as pagan by others. First, there is no model for a prayer labyrinth in the Bible, but there is, as noted earlier, a physical model, arguably, a pathway of prayer, in the tabernacle. Labyrinths are marked garden paths that usually follow a circuitous route to the center of the circle and back out again. It often involves an intricate design that follows a single path – making it unicursal. It is not a maze, a puzzle to be solved, something meant to confuse with its dead ends. On the contrary, a labyrinth is designed so that its path is easily followed to the center.

The cathedral of Chartres, France, has a labyrinth, as does the one in Duomo di Siena, Tuscany. Grace Cathedral, an Episcopal church in San Francisco, maintains two. Labyrinths were embedded as floor patterns in cathedrals in the Middle Ages. One researcher found 22 labyrinths in 80 Middle Age cathedrals. When rationalism seemed to triumph, labyrinths came to be viewed as childish and non-intellectual, so cathedrals tore them out or covered them. As many as a thousand labyrinths have been created in the US; however, most are non-Christian. One reason labyrinths are resisted by evangelicals is their association first with Roman Catholicism and, now, with their use by the Emergent Church, as well as New Agers and neo-pagans.

In some instances, the church suggested the labyrinth as a substitute for a pilgrimage to Jerusalem or as a symbol of the pursuit of God. It is sometimes called a "sacred path" or "gateway." In ancient times, three stages of spiritual development were in view – consecra-

tion (releasing, abandoning, yielding), insight (receiving, appropri-
ating, understanding), and union (returning, redirecting, renewing).
In consecration, one crucifies desires of the world or the flesh and
presses into God. He opens his heart; he is asking, seeking, knocking.
At the center of the labyrinth, illumination comes – theoretically, it is
the point of receiving, of hearing, of listening. As one exits the labyrinth, the focus is on communion with God, union with His will and
purposes. It is joining God in His mission, exiting to serve.

If walking and praying are actions you love to combine, you
might want to use the idea of a labyrinth or prayer stations that
mark certain concepts that you use to consistently reinforce healthy
spirituality. Obviously, as with any prayer practice, you want to avoid
ritualism and superficiality. It isn't a place, it's a person. It is not in
words, it is beyond words. For some folks, walking a pattern designed to help them focus and concentrate in prayer may be helpful;
for others, it could degenerate into a kind of unhealthy legalism.

APPENDIX 3

The Tree of the Knowledge of Good and Evil

The deadly nature of the forbidden tree and its consequences was *experiential* knowledge for which God sought to shield Adam and Eve. He desired their innocence – some things they did not need to know, nor do we. Some things we do not want our children to learn the hard way. We seek to shield them from such experiences. We warn them – so does God. Yahweh here retains the prerogative to impart knowledge as He chooses, specifically, the knowledge of the holy, and His divine prerogative to call evil, evil, and good, good; and, further, to then share, to disclose at His discretion, His secrets to man as He sovereignly chooses. At the heart of the prayer experience, just as these trees were in the center of the garden, is the issue of knowledge – more precisely, how we acquire spiritual knowledge and how we appropriate life. It is the issue of whether or not we trust God – or ourselves, or other voices. "Curiosity," we are warned, "is one of Satan's most dangerous weapons."[87] – specifically, unbounded curiosity.

Much of our praying dances between these two trees – "What about this or that, God?" We pray for life in our finances and families, our churches and cities – life. As we learn from the narrative, the on-going right to partake of the tree of life is dependent on our restraint before the tree of the knowledge of good mixed with, polluted with, evil. Rights and restraint, blessing and boundaries, are in tension one with another. There is no right to both trees.

Experiential knowledge is gained only through experience. Modern liberals now suggest that this is the only means by which any-

---

87 Brooks, Thomas (Kindle Location 2611).

thing can be genuinely known. Priori knowledge is knowledge before experience; it is disclosed knowledge, and, therefore, it is knowledge demanding the trust of another. It may be from observation or from disclosed information, but it is in some way propositional truth, a rational argument we embrace. "I'll take your word for it," we wisely say, and forego the test of veracity. In our culture, we further surmise that if a proposition is not testable, not veritable by empirical data, it cannot be asserted as truth.[88] Such a thesis undermines Biblical revelation and faith itself. Notice, this is no new battle – it surfaces in the Genesis narrative. This rationalism was the effective tool used to interject doubt about God and His word, and highjack man's dominion and precipitate his fall.

---

88 Empirical knowledge, also called "a posterior knowledge", is only acquired through mastery by involvement or exposure. It is knowledge one experiences. Christianity, as does Judaism, demands trust in its God. Eastern religions are ripe with their elevation of experiential knowledge – and that accounts, in part, for their popularity. Zen, for example, emphasizes the experiential element in religious experience as superior to 'the trap of conceptualization.' One Buddhist expression says, "Merely talking about fire does not make the mouth burn!" Anything less than the experience is only theory, only words, only sound. Ultimately, then, God can't know, for example, that sin is really evil, because He has never sinned. Modern psychology and sociology, informed by humanistic relativism, has brought experiential learning to the center, for example, of self-help therapeutic groups – and in many ways, general (lay) or professional knowledge are subordinated to personal experience and perspective. "You can't know how I feel, what I am going through!" This is the exaltation of the personal, the experiential, as the measure of all reality, and it is the essence of relativism – all truth is only the truth that one can know and comes to believe to be true. It is truth affirmed by one's own narrow experiences. Here is Narcissus, trapped in the vision of his own reflection, his own limited experiential knowledge.

APPENDIX 4

Trusting God to Know

The presence of the tree of the knowledge of good and evil in the Genesis narrative is a call for faith in God's *character*, in His word, His disclosures and, ultimately, in His proprietorship of a pool of knowledge beyond the scope of man. At the heart of the prayer experience is the issue of trust. Is our knowing that God knows enough for us? Must we taste the evil that he warns against, learning all our lessons the hard way? Here is the vast difference between the *infinite* knowledge of God and the *finite* knowledge of man – the recognition and acceptance of the great gulf between man the creature, though he was created in God's image, and God, the Creator. Based on such trust, we are to rest, relying on God's disclosures to us, His whisperings to us in the secret place of prayer. Adam and Eve were to restrain themselves. They were to avoid the distraction and temptation of this tree of knowledge. Instead, it became their central focus in the garden of prayer, and they grasped at its answers.

In Genesis 3, trust in God's warning, His word, is at the heart of the temptation. The serpent's thesis was that this priori knowledge of God was not to be trusted, indeed, that God was not to be trusted. *"Did God say to you, 'You shall not eat of every tree of the garden?'"* The serpent appears to have secret knowledge, access to a conversation that took place in his absence – he was 'in the know!' Then he offered a two-fold misrepresentation – first, a charge against the character of God, *"You will not surely die!"* Implying, "What God has told you is not true! Do not trust the priori knowledge." In its most blatant form, the serpent was saying, "God is lying to you!" In its more subtle form, he was appealing to them, "Trust only what you experience, what you come to know as real for yourself" – empirical knowledge. This calls into question God's motives, particularly His character. It also sets forth the proposition that we can only really *know* by experiential knowledge, *"God knows that in the day you eat thereof, your eyes shall be opened..."* The unknowable is knowable, but only by experience. The thesis is twice flawed. Despite man's arrogant assumptions, some things will always be known by God alone; they are knowable only by His gracious disclosures. Further, some things must be experientially avoided – we must 'trust' God in order to 'experience' life itself. Some things we know by trust, others by taste, but it is God who determines the menu.

The serpent theorized, however, that only by the embrace of unbounded sensate experimentation – the hearing, seeing, touching, smelling, tasting, eating and sharing – could enlightenment, the higher knowledge, come. It is an old idea, and it is deadly. Such knowledge, the serpent proposed, was the key to being *a god*. His thesis erased the distance between the finite and the infinite,[89] the mortal and the immortal, the perspective from heaven and that from earth. *"And you shall be as gods"* was and is a false thesis, a delusional promise.

At the healthy center of prayer is always the question of faith in the *character* of God. Prayer requires humility before God, and that means the acceptance of our limitations, our finite nature and trust in God's infiniteness. It means that we rest in the confidence that

---

89 There is a version of prayer that, in a similar way, erases the distinction between God, the infinite, and man, the finite. When we deify prayer, we again erase this line. We tend to speak of the *power* of prayer. In truth, prayer has no power – the power is with God. Prayer is not a power over God, it is a means of experiencing the power of God. Prayer is not sovereign; God is sovereign. When we invert the power dynamic in prayer, we do the same – making God the servant, the fulfiller of our prayer requests, the One who jumps to our 'prayer commands.'

God knows what we don't know, what we may never know, and that God discloses as He wills, and we trust and obey (John 16:13). This place of trust is beyond our own understanding, from our heart more than our head (Prov. 3:4-5). It refuses to *grasp* at what only God has the right to *give* (Phil. 2:6).

APPENDIX 5

The Deadly Absence of Gratitude

Another key to prayer and to understanding the Genesis narrative is found not only in what is present, but also in what is absent. Specifically, gratitude is missing altogether from the Genesis narrative. Adam and Eve were granted life, life in the image of God, dominion and the re-creative capacity never extended to the angelic community. There was so much to be thankful for, but gratitude was not on their lips. G. K. Chesterton called thanks "the highest form of thought," and gratitude..."happiness doubled by wonder." Adam and Eve were in paradise, standing in the middle of a beautiful prayer garden created as a special meeting place with God, and they were without wonder, blind, seeing only what they could not have, what they were forbidden from having – and that for their own good.

Gratitude is the beginning, the first indicator that one has tasted grace. Gratitude and grace are conjoined. With grace, we are amazed, humbled in wonder and awed by God's goodness. Within the grip of grace, we are gently constrained by our own will to obedience. Grateful, we feel a debt to the relationship. Having experienced the bounty, the goodness of God, we are induced to trust. Dietrich Bonhoeffer said, "It is only with gratitude that life becomes rich!" Only with gratitude do we awaken to the riches God has placed in and around our lives. The psalmist called gratitude the gateway into God's presence (100:4). The recurring phrase in the creation narrative is, *"And it was good,"* occurring seven times (Genesis 1:4, 10, 12, 18, 21, 25, 31). But this was not a phrase in the vocabulary of Adam and Eve. They never spoke of the goodness of the God of creation. With ingratitude, the first couple then turned their back on the goodness of God, arguably on His presence, and, in so doing, they were face-to-face with the serpent. In a radical contrast with the way God saw things, Eve saw the tree, with its knowledge of good and evil, as good (3:6). And she and Adam ate.

Ingratitude is the fruit of pride, of a self-centered perspective that views life in the narrow terms of self-interest and personal power. Pride wants no restraint. Pride does not want to depend on another – it is satisfied only with self-reliance. It does not like to bend or bow. It does not like to be second or subordinate. It *"goes before destruction... before a fall"* (Prov. 16:18). Moreover, destruction finds as its cause haughtiness. Humility, on the other hand, issues forth in honor and honorable behavior (Prov. 18:12). Paul says, of fallen men, *"...they knew God, but they glorified him not as God, neither were thankful."* The point can be applied here as well, starting with Adam and Eve, and the result of ingratitude, of withheld worship, of the failure to see all they had been given, corrupted their thinking. They, as we do as well without grateful humility, *"became vain in their imaginations, and their foolish heart was darkened"* (Romans 1:21).

The one certain means of polluting the garden was the appropriation of this forbidden fruit that mixed the knowledge of good and evil.[90] The serpent alleged, *"God knows that your eyes will be opened as soon as you eat it, and you will be like God, knowing both good and evil"* (Gen. 3:8). The same word is used twice – *"God knows"* (yada), *"and you will be like God, knowing"* (yada). The meaning of the phrase has been debated over and over. If God *knows*, then *knowing like* God

---

90 The term *knowledge* here in Hebrew is *daath*, pronounced *dah'-ath*. The phrase good and evil in Hebrew is a literary device used to pair opposite ideas. In the broadest sense, it can mean 'everything' from good to evil. Jewish tradition narrows the meaning from acquisition for general knowledge to the mixture of good and evil together. The tradition of seeing the forbidden fruit as an apple may be related to the word play of *malum*, apple, and *malum*, evil. When evil is internalized, everything changes. Suddenly, the temptation is not external; the inner 'Evil Inclination' emerges. The nature of man's heart has been changed.

knows, arguably, *what* God *knows* – can't be evil. Knowledge itself is not evil! The meaning of the term *yada* often depends on the context.[91] *Yada* has been generously defined as the dedication, the pursuit of the knowledge of another, in order to love them more deeply. Perhaps the tree is simply God's way of saying, "There is a way to know me, and another way that will not lead either to healthy spiritual knowledge or to life." *Yada,* then, is faithfully living out the implications of our covenant relationship with the Lord, based on trust and love,[92] allowing him to set the boundaries of the relationship.

The problem was not some poison in the pulp of the fruit – it was in their self-centered *grasp.* They did not wait for God to 'give them' what was His right to *give,* they *grasped.* They grasped because they believed the lie that God was holding out on them, not being forthright, and keeping them under His thumb. Lucifer had wrongly calculated the distance between himself and God as narrow, as a gap he could close; he aspired to be a god – God! In the garden, he offered the same lie to Adam and Eve, that they could be as gods; and, sadly, they failed to see the vast difference between their being created in the image of God, their being a reflection of His image, and their being gods.

---

91 For example: *"Adam knew [yada] his wife Eve, and she conceived...Cain knew [yada] his wife, and she conceived..."* (Genesis 4:1, 17, see also 25). This is intimate knowledge, and here it implies sexual intimacy. But in a broader sense, *yada* is neither explicitly carnal or sexual.

92 Jeremiah pointed to Josiah as a great king, *"...just and right in all his dealings. That,"* the prophet asserted, *"is why God blessed him. He gave justice and help to the poor and needy, and [as a result] everything went well for him."* Then comes the question, *"Isn't that what it means to know [yada] me?"* (Jeremiah 22:15-16). Here is the issue of the kind of knowledge, the kind of life perspective, which treats others in sensitive ways. Proverbs 12:10 says, *"The righteous know [yada] the needs of their animals, but the mercy of the wicked is cruel."* Yada, then, is a kind of knowledge that leads to the sensitivity and care of God's creation. A good person is a caring person – even to animals – and the evil man is insensitive, he shows no mercy. In yet another passage, yada means to act justly, righteously. To know the Lord, then, is to do justice, to show mercy to those less fortunate, to exemplify a godly and righteous character.

Grasping. Doubting. Disregarding the sacred boundaries. Failing to trust. Not being grateful for all they had been given. Not worshipping. Ignoring God, and opening a dialogue with the serpent – what else could go wrong?[93]

---

93 *"Wisdom,"* not knowledge, the writer of Proverbs says, *"…is a tree of life to those who embrace her; happy are those who hold her tightly"* (Prov. 3:18). Knowledge answers 'what' questions, it is superficial at best; wisdom answers 'why' questions, and that goes to motive. Wisdom, as every student of Proverbs knows, is a metaphor for God Himself – He is 'Wisdom.' Some say the reference is to God, the Holy Spirit, who discloses divine secrets. Isaiah calls the *"Spirit of the LORD… the Spirit of wisdom and of understanding,"* as well as the *"Spirit of the knowledge and fear of the LORD"* (Isa. 11:12). Here, knowledge reverences, fears God – the opposite of the action in the Genesis narrative. The serpent proposes an access to superior knowledge apart from God. Obviously, apart from the revelation by the Spirit – he, the serpent, Lucifer, offers his tutoring services. This is far removed from the pathway to wisdom that begins with the fear of God.

If the word "pray" is used 313 times in the Word of God, it must be an imperative—that of expressing a command in a forceful and confident way. Doug Small has taken praying to a higher level of influence with the Schools of Prayer. To really experience change, involve your church with multiple churches in your area for greater impact of the prayer implementation. Prayer changes people and people change the world! Acts 4:31 ... "And when they had prayed, the place was shaken!"

Dr. Timothy M. Hill, Director
Church of God World Missions

I first met Doug Small at a Heart-Cry for Revival conference. I immediately began to see his heart and passion for prayer and unity. Having shared speaking times with him at a Revival forum and seeing his strategy for praying for a city, was revolutionary. His ability to speak across denominational lines to the things that should unite it rather than the secondary things that can divide us, was a great encouragement to me.

Pastor Michael Catt, Lead Pastor
Sherwood Baptist, Albany, GA

Doug Small brings an engaging, energetic, and Holy Spirit sensitive voice to the body of Christ. The Holy Spirit is using him to connect Christians from across denominational lines and bring us back to a fresh understanding of our unity in Christ. Doug's passion for righteousness stirs my heart to prayer for our nation and world.

Dr. Doug Beacham, General Superintendent
International Pentecostal Holiness Church

Doug Small is a highly respected national prayer leader with a passion for bringing a fresh air of prayer to the local church. He equips through a powerful mix of biblical and practical teaching with strategic and prophetic insights. More than a seminar of notes and quotes, Doug creates a transformative spiritual experience for any church eager to become prayer-driven for the Gospel of Jesus Christ.

Phil Miglioratti,
Mission America Coalition, National Facilitator

When our organization wanted someone who understood how to foster a culture of powerful prayer, we turned to Doug Small. He brought biblical, Christ-exalting messages coupled with a winsome spirit and presentation. If you long to ignite lasting impact in your congregation, Doug is a spiritual flame-starter!

Byron Paulus, President,
Life Action Ministries

TOPICS

- Why Study the Tabernacle?
- How Many Tabernacles Were There?
- Introducing the Tabernacle of Moses
- Taking a Tour of the Tabernacle
- The Gate—the Principle of Praise
- The Brazen Altar—the Principle of Sacrifice
- The Offerings of Consecration
- The Offerings of Reparation
- The Sacrifices—an Application
- The Laver—the Principle of Sanctification
- The Holy Place—the Principle of the Deeper Life
- The Lampstand
- The Table—the Principle of Balance
- The Altar of Incense—the Principle of Communion With God
- Beyond the Veil—the Principle of Reverence
- The Most Holy Place—the Principle of Reverence
- The Ark of the Covenant—the Principles of His Covenant
- Exiting to Serve—the Principle of Transformation

www.alivepublications.org

THE

PRAYING CHURCH

HANDBOOK

- *A collection of substantive reflections on prayer.*
- *Contributors include global and national leaders, as well as Church of God authors, leaders and intercessors.*
- *The chapters are sprinkled with prayer quotes, and interjected with prayer vignettes.*
- *Volume I - Foundations, Volume II - Personal and Family Prayer, Volume III - The Pastor and the Congregation are now available.*
- *The completed set will include 4 volumes. The 4th volume, Intercessory Prayer and Mission will be released in 2016.*

www.alivepublications.org

THE
PRAYING
CHURCH
HANDBOOK

A Companion to
The Praying Church Resource Guide

VOLUME I — FOUNDATIONS

THE
PRAYING
CHURCH
HANDBOOK

A Companion to
The Praying Church Resource Guide

VOLUME II — PERSONAL AND
FAMILY PRAYER

THE
PRAYING
CHURCH
HANDBOOK

A Companion to
The Praying Church Resource Guide

VOLUME III — THE PASTOR AND
THE CONGREGATION

"I can't believe how this has changed my prayer life."

Host a
School of Prayer with P. Douglas Small

Schools of Prayer are seminars structured around learning and experiencing prayer.
Topics include:

- Enriching Your Personal Prayer Life
- Praying Through the Tabernacle
- Prayer the Heartbeat of the Church
- Heaven is a Courtroom
- Theology and Philosophy for Prayer Ministry
- Organizing Intercessors
- Entertaining God
- The Critical Strategic Uncomfortable Middle

PROJECT
PRAY

www.projectpray.org
1-855-84-ALIVE